P9-CCP-733

"According to Ms. Crittenden's perceptive critique, the thing these mothers didn't tell their daughters, which every previous generation had known instinctively, is that they have bodies and thus natures. These natures would cause them to crave, as they matured, not only autonomy but children, family, companionship and love. She argues incisively that disregarding this simple truth has made the daughters' generation less happy."
—Francis Fukuyama, *The Wall Street Journal*

"Danielle Crittenden writes with passion, persuasiveness, and uncommon sense. When they are older and confronting the challenges of adolescence and adulthood, I expect, my own daughters will be able to benefit from this eloquent and important book."
—Michael Medved, nationally syndicated radio host and author of *Saving Childhood: Protecting Our Children from the National Assault on Innocence*

"Danielle Crittenden urges women to rediscover fulfillment. . . . Such ancient advice is revolutionary today."
—Suzanne Fields, *Los Angeles Times Syndicate*

"*What Our Mothers Didn't Tell Us* is a scintillating guide for young women through the minefield of sexual politics. With humor and unsparing common sense, Crittenden describes the perils of postponing marriage, postponing childbirth, dating in your thirties. One need not agree with her on every point to derive enormous benefits from her message. To ignore her caveats is to seriously diminish one's prospects for life with a decent man and well-cared-for children."
—Christina Hoff Sommers, author of *Who Stole Feminism?*

"Lively and provocative. . . . Crittenden does not suggest that women give up their dreams for marriage, family, and fulfilling work; just that they better plan for and prioritize all the different aspects of life they hope to experience."
—Betsy Hart, *Chicago Sun-Times*

"[Crittenden] has just detonated a grenade in the face of the women's movement."
—Joanna Coles, *The Times of London*

"One is likely to be charmed by the witty, elegant prose, and either moved or provoked by the ideas—maybe both. [Crittenden] puts her finger on genuine anxieties: about marriage and family roles, careers and children. . . . As they ponder their life choices, young women would do well to consider many of the points raised in this book. . . ."
—Cathy Young, *The Philadelphia Inquirer*

"If wicked wit and careful reflection don't grab you, Danielle Crittenden will sweep you along with her incontrovertible logic."
—Mona Charen, *The Detroit News*

"With wit and style, Danielle Crittenden shatters the tired clichés of bitter feminists and brilliantly explores the classic truths and modern realities that women confront."
—Kate O'Beirne, Washington editor, *National Review*

Danielle Crittenden

What Our Mothers

Why Happiness Eludes

Didn't Tell Us

the Modern Woman

A Touchstone Book

Published by Simon & Schuster

New York London

Sydney Singapore

TOUCHSTONE
Rockefeller Center
1230 Avenue of the Americas
New York, NY 10020

Copyright © 1999 by Danielle Crittenden
All rights reserved,
including the right of reproduction
in whole or in part in any form.
First Touchstone Edition 2000

TOUCHSTONE and colophon are registered trademarks
of Simon & Schuster, Inc.

Designed by Jeanette Olender
Manufactured in the United States of America

3 5 7 9 10 8 6 4

The Library of Congress has cataloged the Simon & Schuster edition as follows:
Crittenden, Danielle, 1963-
What our mothers didn't tell us : why happiness eludes
the modern woman / Danielle Crittenden.
p. cm.
Includes index.
1. Women—United States—Social conditions.
2. Women—United States—Psychology. 3. Feminism—United States.
4. Sex role—United States. I. Title.
HQ1421.C75 1999
305.42'0973—dc21 98-42580
CIP
ISBN 0-684-83219-4
0-684-85959-9 (PBK)

For my mother

Contents

Acknowledgments

MY MOTHER told me quite a lot, actually—and taught me even more by her example. Very few of the ideas in this book could be asserted quite so confidently without her inspiration as a mother, journalist, wife, and grandmother. Thanks must be paid as well to the angel who thoughtfully dropped my stepfather, Peter Worthington, into my life at an early age: He has not simply been the best, most encouraging, and generous of fathers, but a model of intellectual courage and journalistic integrity.

I've also had the good fortune to marry into a family of modern-day heroines whose own lives have been enviably full, fascinating, and exemplary: Florence Rosberg and my late mother-in-law Barbara Frum. Their thoughts and perspective on the "woman question" have aided me greatly.

I thank my agent, Kris Dahl, and my two persistent editors, Laurie Chittenden and Cynthia Gitter, who worked hard to get this book published and whose opinions and suggestions have been invaluable. Invaluable, too, has been the help and comradeship of Grace Paine Terzian and Mitzi Hamilton, and the assistance of Rhonda K. Mohrmann. I'm indebted to the support of Anita Blair, Heather Higgins, Barbara Ledeen, Elizabeth Lurie, and Ricky Silberman of the Independent Women's Forum; to the IWF for providing me with the vehicle of *The Women's Quarterly* and the unparalleled editorial freedom to drive it wherever I pleased; and to those who financed *The Women's Quarterly*'s often hairraising rides, especially the William H. Donner Foundation.

I'm grateful to have had the honor to work and converse with so many women who have broken ground for ideas expressed in this book, and some who were paving the road long before I ever veered on to it, among them Mona Charen, Midge Decter, Maggie Gallagher, Anne Roche Muggeridge, Kate O'Beirne, Lisa Schiffren, Wendy Shalit, Melinda Ledden Sidak, and Christina Hoff Sommers. Karlyn Bowman of the American Enterprise Institute has been a patient provider and interpreter of poll information. I owe much to the friendships and/or professional encouragement of Barbara Amiel Black, David Brooks, Erich Eichman, Tim Ferguson, John Fraser, Dean Godson, Ernest Hillen, Mildred Istona, Melanie Kirkpatrick, William Kristol, Mary Matalin, Mary Mohler, Barbara Moon, Bob Newman, Anna Porter, Amity Shlaes, Dianna Symonds, David Warren, and George Will. I hope my late father, Max Crittenden, would have been pleased with this book.

I especially thank my children, Miranda and Nathaniel, for the crash course in motherhood that they have given me. Their impatience for me to come downstairs and have some fun kept me in their world, and their wonderfully frank and useful observations about the sexes aided me in mine.

Above all, I wish to thank my husband, David Frum, the cheerful Atlas whose love and strength sustain me. He has had to endure more discussions about the Woman Problem than, I think, Freud himself. Every page has benefited from his wisdom, and every moment in my life from his companionship. "My love for you is deathless. It seems to bind me with mighty cables that nothing but omnipotence can break."

What Our Mothers Didn't Tell Us

*You may drive out nature with a pitchfork,
yet she will still hurry back.*

HORACE

What Our Mothers Didn't Tell Us

NOT LONG ago I found myself sitting at a restaurant table with the editors of a glossy women's magazine. They were three ladies in their early to mid-forties wearing power suits and slightly scuffed pumps. They'd brought along blank notepads and slender pencils and were waiting, flatteringly, to jot down my thoughts on the state of modern womanhood.

Their interest had been piqued by a story I'd written for *The Wall Street Journal* about magazines like theirs. Women today enjoy unprecedented freedom and opportunity. So why, I'd wondered, were the articles in women's magazines so relentlessly pessimistic? I'd pulled thirty years' worth of back issues of *Mademoiselle, Glamour, Vogue, Redbook, Cosmopolitan,* and *McCall's* from the stacks of the Library of Congress. It was partly from reading magazines like these that Betty Friedan had concluded in 1963 that the women of her generation felt unhappy and stifled. A huge social transformation had taken place between Friedan's day and mine. Had it made women any happier? I wasn't looking to the magazines for a scientific answer, of course, just a general gauge of mood. From that perspective, the answer was, resoundingly, no. In fact, these magazines portrayed my contemporaries as even more miserable and insecure, more thwarted and obsessed with men, than the most depressed, Valium-popping, suburban reader of the 1950s.

This wasn't altogether surprising. The longings and passions of human beings don't change much from generation to generation. Women's preoccupation with love and their looks is part of the eternal female condition that no political movement could ever change. But what *was* surprising was the sudden and stark descent from the ebullience and optimism of the dawning of the modern women's movement these magazines celebrated in the early 1970s to the disappointment and bitterness you see in them today. In 1973—the year of the Supreme Court's *Roe* v. *Wade* decision and the Senate's vote to adopt the Equal Rights Amendment to the Constitution—once-demure publications like *McCall's* and *Mademoiselle* were ripping off their pearl necklaces to don the neck scarves of revolutionaries. Men, the magazines trumpeted, would soon be rendered irrelevant. Male reproductive functions would be replaced by artificial insemination. Husbands and lovers would no longer be needed for economic support or companionship (female friends were better, it was agreed) or even sexual pleasure (*Mademoiselle* went so far as to equate dating and marriage with prostitution; in another article it asked, "Is Everybody Basically Bisexual?"). These radical notions were conveyed in the magazines' customary playful manner ("How to Liberate Your Entire Family!"), making them seem deliciously fun, a lark, like indulging in a pair of the season's impractical platform shoes. And they were artfully sandwiched between photo spreads showing gorgeous ways to decorate your new (very own!) apartment, profiles of women who had shunned marriage and motherhood for dazzling careers, and tips for leading a sizzling and adventurous sex life (because men, when they were not being discarded, were to be used as casually as they had once used you).

As I worked my way through this pile of blindingly colorful magazines in the dignified atmosphere of the library's reading room, I was reminded of the day I discovered an orange suede micro-miniskirt hanging in the back of my mother's closet. "How could you have worn this?" I asked her, holding it against my waist. She shrugged: "It was the sixties." The women's magazines of the 1990s likewise shrugged off their old enthusiasms. Having your own apartment has ceased to be novel, and nowadays it's unlikely that you're going to invite a man you've just met home for sex—that is, assuming you are able to meet a man at all. For if there is one attitude that unites the women's magazines of today, it is their pessimism about their readers' love lives. Editors—particularly those of publications aimed at women in their twenties—now seem to take for granted a readership that is whiling away a lot of solitary evenings at the gym. When the magazines are not terrifying women into celibacy with articles on the dangers of "date rape" and sexually transmitted diseases, they are offering desperate "tips" to catch a man's attention ("Spill a drink on him!" suggested *Cosmo*). And once you have managed to turn a man's head, it's assumed that you will have no end of trouble keeping it pivoted in your direction ("Will He Cheat?" asked *Glamour.* "What Are Your Chances of Staying Married?" And so on). If these women's magazines are any indicator, rather than losing all their value in women's eyes—as the liberationists had predicted—men have instead seen their stock skyrocket and split two or three times. In some instances, the very same editors who had urged their readers to walk away from men twenty years ago are now, like crazed commodities traders caught short in a bull market, urging women to snatch them back up at almost any price. In an issue of *Cosmo* from 1989, I came across an alarming, if unscientific, report on the nation's "man shortage." For the romantically desperate, there was a map showing the cities where the male population outnumbered the female; *Cosmo* also helpfully included job prospects, cost-of-living indexes, and profiles of the local economies. A lonely woman was urged to pack up and move to Ames, Iowa, or Gainesville, Florida, the two most promising places. "Much of the archery equipment used in the U.S. is made in Gainesville—increasing chances you'll be hit by one of Cupid's arrows!"

And to snuff out the last flickering source of consolation, editors no longer promise that romantic disappointments can be assuaged by career satisfaction. By the late 1970s, the magazines had ceased to regard the workplace as an exciting unexplored frontier. They now describe the office as just another source of frustration and boredom—that is, when it's not a venue for sexual harassment, or the cause of the exhaustion and distress of working mothers.

What happened?

This was what the editors who had invited me to lunch wanted to know. As their pencils hovered and our plates arrived, I was nervously aware that my opinion on the subject was not exactly the stuff of upbeat headlines ("Ten Reasons Why the Modern Woman Is Unhappy and What to *Do* About It!"). Indeed, as I began to explain how I thought the unhappiness expressed in the magazines' pages was the inevitable outcome of certain feminist beliefs, I saw disappointment cross the editors' faces. They discreetly put down their pencils and sipped their mineral water. When at last they responded, it became clear that what they hoped I'd offer them was not a criticism of feminism but rather a positive indication of where the women's movement should, as they put it, "go next." It was true, the editors agreed, that some feminists lately had gone "too far," and polls suggested the majority of women curled away from the word *feminist* as if it were a rotting substance found at the back of the fridge. But that didn't mean, the editors insisted, that we should abandon feminism entirely. We just needed to polish up its image—find "the new Gloria Steinem," who could market some improved brand of feminism, one that might appeal to the millions of young women who seemed uninterested in the whole subject.

In some ways, the editors' unwavering belief in the power of feminism was inspiring. Feminism was their faith. It was as feminists that they had come of age; it was feminism that had defined their identities as women. Its failures and disappointments were no reason to give it up; to the contrary, they were the reason to press forward more keenly than ever. As they listened to me, first with bafflement, then with irritation, and finally with anger, I thought of an apparatchik I'd met in Slovakia shortly after the collapse of Communism in Eastern Europe. He was still occupying an office in a government building in central Bratislava. He had not been fired because he wasn't perceived as one of the "bad" Communists: In his years of work for the municipal bureaucracy, he'd sent no one to prison, and had even modernized the city's plumbing. He was bewildered by the popular rejection of an ideology he'd spent his entire life implementing and still fervently believed in. How would the masses live without it? he fretted. What would protect them from unbridled capitalism and American cultural imperialism? So too these magazine editors could not imagine a society in which feminism did not reign over the minds of women, or at the very least over those who hold political and judicial power. Without feminism, they feared, we were in danger of "going back"—back to what, exactly, was never spelled out because to them it was self-evidently terrible. Domestic servitude? Beehive hairdos? Might we even lose the vote?

IT'S COMMON now for the elders of the women's movement to express disappointment in my generation of women—the "daughters of the revolution" now in their twenties and thirties—who came of age long after the last feminist brassiere had been burned. As they see it, we are enjoying the spoils of their victories without any gratitude for their struggle. We get up in the morning and go to our jobs as doctors, executives, plumbers, soldiers without devoting a second's thought to the efforts that were spent making these jobs seem completely normal. We deposit our paychecks without having to worry whether we are getting paid less for the job we're doing because of our sex. We enroll in science courses with every expectation of being taken seriously as scientists; we apply for postgraduate degrees with every expectation that we will use them and not let them languish when we become mothers. When we graduate, our first thought is not, Whom will I marry? but, What will I do? And when we do marry, we take for granted that our husbands will treat us as equals, with dreams and ambitions like theirs, and not as creatures uniquely destined to push a vacuum or change a diaper. If Virginia Woolf, in the early part of this century, modestly hoped that women would attain "rooms of our own," we have, at century's end, not only achieved rooms of our own but apartments of our own, offices of our own, bank accounts of our own, judicial seats of our own, constituencies of our own, and even corporate empires of our own.

In that sense we are enjoying the spoils of our elders' struggles. But if we seem ungrateful, or indifferent, it is not because we don't believe in the ideas that were bequeathed to us. Just a few months before my lunch with the magazine editors, I'd spent some time driving around colleges in the Northeast—small elite schools like Smith and Yale and larger state schools like the University of Massachusetts—talking to female students for another article I was writing. I was curious to know what (if anything) feminism meant to women who had grown up in a world long altered by the activism of their mothers. While it was true that most of the students I spoke to—women who said they were going to be doctors and lawyers, professors and bankers—declined to describe themselves as "feminist" ("I'm not sure what that word means anymore" was the usual explanation given), every opinion they expressed would have warmed the heart of the most fiery "libber" a quarter century ago. A twenty-year-old Ivy League student said that she was planning to have children outside of marriage because she feared a husband might "threaten her individuality." Another told me that she had stopped dating a man she loved because neither one of them was willing to make concessions to the other's career plans. With few exceptions, the students expressed quite casual attitudes about sex. They spoke of their affairs with detachment and became passionate only when discussing their ex-lovers' reluctance to do the dishes. Virtually every young woman I interviewed put her job aspirations ahead of any hopes for marriage or children (even if she claimed to want those things eventually). Each one of them worried that too serious an attachment to a man or, worse, to children might compromise her sense of who she was.

Few of these students had read Betty Friedan's *The Feminine Mystique* or other feminist classics. Only a handful had joined the campus women's groups. It didn't matter. Their generation had provided the laboratory mice for the social experiments of the past twenty-five years. They had grown up with working mothers, day care, and no-fault divorce. Their primary school textbooks were illustrated with little girls flying planes and little boys mopping the floors. They took coed classes in shop and metalworking instead of home economics. They'd participated in frank discussions about birth control and sexuality with their grade-school teachers. Their developing intellects had been bombarded by feminist cultural messages: the proudly menstruating heroines of Judy Blume novels, the supportive articles about single mothers in the lifestyle sections of newspapers, the applause on daytime talk shows for women who divorce their husbands in order to "realize themselves." The students I interviewed had neither adopted nor rejected feminism. Rather, it had seeped into their minds like intravenous saline into the arm of an unconscious patient. They were feminists without knowing it.

Indeed, when I sought out those who did consciously and proudly call themselves feminists, I usually found myself on the fringes of student society, among women with odd personalities and carefully cultivated grievances: lesbians who had moved out of the dormitories to form separatist communes; women's studies majors who, like the Marxists of the 1930s, had undergone an almost religious conversion and now spoke about even the weather in stark, ideological terms; activists who would protest anything from the cruelty of chicken farming to the patriarchal tyranny of English grammar and punctuation. I remember arriving to interview the head of one university's women's center—the feminist gathering places that are now as common on college campuses as sports arenas—only to find a young woman dressed from head to toe in black, lying in the middle of the floor surrounded by half-finished signs for an upcoming demonstration. Her hair was dyed bright green and styled as if by electric shock. As she sleepily came to (she was hung over, it turned out), she described herself as being "a socialist feminist, I guess, but really I'm all over the place—Marxist, radical—but not anywhere near liberal feminism" (a phrase she pronounced with contempt). Women who did not see the conspiracy mounted against them by "the patriarchy," she said wearily, were just "so f—ing passive."

It is because women like these call themselves feminists that so many others have decided that feminism has gone "too far." But in their own way, these extremists also embody feminism's success. Ideas that once seemed radical—whether it was equal pay for equal work, or rebelling against housework and marriage, or storming boardrooms and military academies—have been so completely absorbed by our society and accepted by its institutions all the way up to the Supreme Court that the only way left to be truly radical is to become a nut.

Still, leaders of the women's movement will frequently say that the success women have achieved is not enough. They warn us that the same forces that brought about our oppression could rise again or *are* on the rise again. Thus, in 1996, the fantastically successful female editor of *The New Yorker* could put together a special issue on women that, in one gulp, left the reader with the impression that to be a modern woman is to live in constant danger of rape, wrongful imprisonment, "patriarchal atrocity," lascivious bosses, right-wing zealotry, and murder on the job. Thus the new feminists like Susan Faludi and Naomi Wolf can argue, to a largely credulous press, that women are being brainwashed back into the 1950s by a male-dominated media and its female stooges or that women diet and wear eye shadow because they unthinkingly accept the impossible beauty standards of the (again) male-dominated advertising industry. Thus feminist organizations can float unsubstantiated whoppers like "wife battery escalates on Super Bowl Sunday" and not one reporter pauses to question the statistic before it has been broadcast across the country. Thus the legal definition of sexual harassment can be stretched to include a bungled pass or an undesired compliment.

And this is what those women's magazines I waded through that day in the library so vividly reflected. Their readers, no matter how depressed or thwarted the articles indicated they felt, are not depressed or thwarted in the same way their mothers were. The women who buy these magazines today have heeded their mothers' advice: *Do something with your life; don't depend upon a man to take care of you; don't make the same mistakes I did.* So they have made different mistakes. They are the women who postponed marriage and childbirth to pursue their careers only to find themselves at thirty-five still single and baby-crazy, with no husband in sight. They are the unwed mothers who now depend upon the state to provide what the fathers of their children won't—a place to live and an income to support their kids. They are the eighteen-year-old girls who believed they could lead the unfettered sexual lives of men, only to end up in an abortion clinic or attending grade twelve English while eight months' pregnant. They are the new brides who understand that when a couple promises to stay together forever, they have little better than a fifty-fifty chance of sticking to it. They are the female partners at law firms who thought they'd made provisions for everything about their career—except for that sudden, unexpected moment when they find their insides shredding the first day they return from maternity leave, having placed their infants in a stranger's arms. They are the young mothers who quit their jobs to be with their babies and who now feel anxiety and even a mild sense of embarrassment about what they have chosen to do— who look over their fences at the quiet backyards of two-career couples, wondering if they haven't done a foolish thing, and feeling a kind of isolation their mothers never knew. Above all, these women are the majority of us, women who are hoping to do everything—work, children, marriage—only to ask ourselves why the pieces haven't added up the way we'd like or why we are collapsing under the strain of it all and doing everything so badly.

The urgent and compelling questions that haunt us from moment to moment are ones to which the women's movement offers no answers— or, when it does, answers that are unhelpful. Is work really more important and fulfilling than raising my children? Why does my boyfriend not want to get married as much as I do? Why is the balance between being a good mother and working so elusive? Why could my mother afford to stay home with her children while I cannot? By giving up my job, am I giving up my identity? Should men and women be trying to lead identical kinds of lives, or were there good reasons for the old divisions of labor between mother and father, husband and wife? If so, do these divisions make us "unequal"?

In a way, the situation women wake up in today is more dire than the one of thirty years ago, when Friedan first sat down to write about the gnawing "problem with no name." For unlike the problem about which Friedan spoke—which afflicted educated suburban wives trapped and unfulfilled in their well-upholstered ranch homes—this new problem with no name affects the female executive high atop the city in her glass office as much as the single mother struggling to lift a stroller onto a bus thirty storeys below. Despite sweeping government programs, tens of billions of dollars in social spending, and massive social upheaval in the name of sexual equality, you only have to glance through a newspaper or switch on the news to be subject to a litany of gloomy statistics about today's women: We are more likely to be divorced or never married at all than women of previous generations. We are more likely to bear children out of wedlock. We are more likely to be junkies or drunks or to die in poverty. We are more likely to have an abortion or to catch a sexually transmitted disease. If we are mothers, even of infants and very small children, we are more likely to work at full-time jobs and still shoulder the bulk of housework as well.

These troubling indicators of female distress are debated at election time and elaborately discussed in the press. But all too often they are treated as a hundred distinct issues. Yet just as Friedan recognized that the million individual breakdowns and lithium addictions taking place in American suburbs indicated a more general problem among women, so must this modern problem with no name be recognized. In Friedan's time, the problem was that too many people failed to see that while women were women, they were also human, and they were being denied the ability to express and fulfill their human potential outside the home. The modern problem with no name is, I believe, exactly the reverse of the old one: While we now recognize that women are human, we blind ourselves to the fact that we are also women. If we feel stunted and oppressed when denied the chance to realize our human potential, we suffer every bit as much when cut off from those aspects of life that are distinctly and uniquely female.

Those aspects of life—whether it's the pleasure of being a wife or of raising children or of making a home—were, until the day before yesterday, considered the most natural things in the world. After all, our grandmothers didn't agonize over such existential questions as to whether marriage was ultimately "right" for them as women or if having a baby would "compromise" them as individuals. Yet we do. We approach these aspects of life warily and self-consciously: A new bride adjusts her veil in the mirror and frets that she is selling out to some false idea of femininity; a new wife is horrified to find herself slipping into the habit of cooking dinner and doing the laundry; a new mother, who has spent years climbing the corporate ladder, is thrown into an identity crisis when she's stuck at home day after day, in a sweatsuit, at the mercy of a crying infant. It is because of feminism's success that we now call these parts of our lives into question, that we don't thoughtlessly march down the aisle, take up our mops, and suppress our ambitions. But feminism, for all its efforts, hasn't been able to banish fundamental female desires from us, either—and we simply cannot be happy if we ignore them.

For if we, as women, were all to sit down and honestly attempt to figure out what sort of lives *would* make us happy, I suspect—assuming the basics like food and adequate income and leaving aside fantasies of riches and celebrity—that most of our answers would be very similar to one another's, and quite different from men's. They would go something like this: We want to marry husbands who will love and respect us; we want to have children; we want to be good mothers. At the same time, many of us will want to pursue interests outside of our families, interests that will vary from woman to woman, depending upon her ambition and talent. Some women will be content with work or involvements that can be squeezed in around their commitments at home; some women will want or need to work at a job, either full- or part-time. Other women will be more ambitious—they may want to be surgeons or corporate executives or lawyers or artists. For them, the competing demands of family and work will always be difficult to resolve. But I think when we compare our conditions for happiness, most of our lists would share these essentials: husband, children, home, work. (The Roper Starch polling firm has asked American women every few years since 1974 about their preferences for marriage, children, and career. The poll conducted in 1995 shows that the majority of women—55 percent—hope to combine all three, and a further 26 percent want marriage and children but *not* a career.) The women who don't desire these things—those who like living alone or who find perfectly fulfilling the companionship of their friends and cats or whose work eclipses their need for family—may be sincerely happy, but they should not be confused with the average woman.

Unfortunately, that confusion is now the prevailing wisdom, one that has been advocated—and continues to be advocated—by the most vocal and influential women's groups. For nearly thirty years, the public policies and individual ways of life that feminists have encouraged, and the laws they have pushed through, have been based on their adamant belief that women want more than equality with men or options outside their families; they want full independence from husbands and family. This is why the "solutions" we hear proposed by these feminists so dramatically fail to appeal to the majority of women. Abortion on demand and condoms in the classroom have failed to prevent millions of unmarried teenagers from becoming mothers before they're old enough to vote. Affirmative action may have propelled some women through the executive ranks, but it has done little for the vast numbers of women who build their work around their family obligations. "No-fault divorce" and other sex-blind laws have perversely punished women, whose special circumstances no longer receive special consideration. Generous welfare benefits to single mothers and shrill warnings about male violence have not dissuaded most women from wanting to share their lives with men. The most liberal family-leave policies cannot begin to address the day-to-day madness that drives so many working women into the ground, nor does "cheaper and better child care" seem any sort of answer to mothers who are already guilt-ridden and concerned about leaving their babies every morning.

It is at this intimate level that feminism has failed women, and maybe no group of women more completely than those who became the very models of feminist achievement. The women who now leave their families every morning to board commuter trains—the women who have traded in their housecoats for business suits, vacuums for computers, carpeted and upholstered living rooms for carpeted and upholstered offices, demanding, tantrum-throwing children for demanding, tantrum-throwing colleagues—may well wonder if they haven't simply traded in one form of unhappiness for another. After all, it should strike us as strange, given the freedom we now enjoy, that happiness should continue to be so elusive. Yet to achieve the very reasonable list of "essentials" that I mentioned previously, all in some sort of balance, seems, for millions of women, as probable as stumbling across the Holy Grail.

This isn't to say there are no solutions to the new problems. To find them, however, will require a new way of thinking about modern women's lives. To do that we must begin by accepting that our problems originate not in our oppression but, as the writer Midge Decter has wisely observed, in our new freedom. And that new freedom *is* a great accomplishment. Yet if we are to enjoy it, and not be defeated by it, we must learn to think in ways quite unlike the ways that feminism has taught us to think. We must reconsider some of the assumptions that have brought us to our current impasse. This does not mean nostalgically wishing to "go back"—as if that were even possible—but it certainly does mean *looking* back, honestly, at what we may have lost in pursuit of the freedom we have won, and asking ourselves whether there is any way to recapture what was good in the old ways we cast aside.

For in all the ripping down of barriers that has taken place over a generation, we may have inadvertently also smashed the foundations necessary for our happiness. Pretending that we are the same as men—with similar needs and desires—has only led many of us to find out, brutally, how different we really are. In demanding radical independence—from men, from our families—we may have also abandoned certain bargains and institutions that didn't always work perfectly but until very recently were civilization's best ways of taming the feckless human heart.

There are a great many women unhappy because they acted upon the wisdom passed along to them by the people they most trusted. These women thought they did everything right—only to have it turn out all wrong. That the wisdom they received was faulty, that it was based on false assumptions, is a hard lesson for anyone to learn. But it is a lesson every woman growing up today will have to learn—as I, and thousands upon thousands of women of my generation, had to learn, often painfully. In this book I can't offer women, as I couldn't the magazine editors, any simple ten-point plan for making our lives easier. But I can sketch out what the new problems are and pinpoint some of the wrong assumptions that created them. So many of us are in the habit of approaching our problems as those arising from inequality and sexism that we cannot imagine any other way to think about them. But we must, urgently, begin to do so. For if we are ever to resolve these problems and take advantage of our new freedoms, we are going to have to look them squarely in the face, unhampered by ideology, and not shy away from what we see.

chapter one

About Sex

IN RETROSPECT, it's almost quaint the way our teachers attempted to teach us about sex. Other generations may have been left to grapple with this most intimate of topics in the dark. We post–baby boomers would be the first to be educated in the subject in public school classrooms in the full light of day. At my high school, the task fell to a gym teacher, who was also the football coach. He was not, even at the best of times, an articulate man.

This wasn't usually a problem: Most of what he needed to say could be grunted or shouted at a field of adolescents, ordering them to tackle, kick, or run around until they threw up. Unfortunately for him, he found himself—like everyone else in the 1970s—at the forefront of sexual enlightenment. Believing that such critical knowledge as birth control and the functions of our sex organs could not be trusted to our stammering and embarrassed parents, education officials passed the duty along to this stammering and embarrassed gym teacher. Why it had to be the gym teacher I'm not sure—perhaps because those same officials hoped to keep the topic safely within the realm of the athletic and away from the romantic. That's also probably why they entitled the sex curriculum "Health" or some similar euphemism (as opposed to "Fellatio 101"), and our textbook spoke about "intercourse" completely matter-of-factly, as if it were no more controversial than the digestive system.

Of course it was—and is. The gym teacher knew it and we knew it. I remember him vividly, standing at the front of the classroom in his red Adidas track suit, grimly tapping a pointer at a full-color diagram of an enormous, bisected vagina. "So, uh, girls have ovaries, right? [tap, tap] And in their ovaries they have, um, ovum, which are tiny eggs. They travel along here [pointer follows strands of red ribbon to something that looks like a cross-section of a bloodied pear] and, uh, sort of nest in here after they've been, um, fertilized by the sperm." The teacher would attempt to deliver these lectures like a Soviet minister addressing the United Nations—monotonously, without any flicker of emotion. We'd try not to snicker. Sometimes it became too acute—his discomfort or our amusement. Suddenly he'd explode and eject some offending boy into the hall with a shouted "You're outta here!"—the way he'd cut a kid from a team. This action would relieve him and restore, briefly, his composure as coach. He'd roll his shoulders and toss a piece of chalk in his palm while glancing down at the binder of course notes.

"Okay, let's move on to masturbation." More sputters of laughter, more ejections, and then the awkward continuation of the class until, mercifully, the bell rang. Most of the time, though, we found the course excruciatingly boring and would marvel at our teacher's ability to make even this subject dull. The names of the various tubes, the journey of the fertilized egg, the average sperm population—all of this could seem as tedious as any geography lesson on the major rivers and cities of South America. Alas, as with geography, we'd face a written exam at the end of the term, so we'd better pay attention: *Name four types of contraception. The ovum is fertilized when (fill in the blank). The tip of the penis is called a) the foreskin; b) the head; c) the sheath; d) none of the above.* If you weren't having sex by fourteen, you almost expected to fail gym.

What we didn't understand at the time—what we couldn't understand—was the underlying goal of the curriculum. As students, we were often told by our teachers to write down and memorize seemingly pointless bits of information. If they decided one day that we should be able to recite all the official mottoes of the various states, we'd yawn and do it, just as we'd done with the distinctions among types of beetles and the molecular composition of Jell-O. Now they wanted to teach us about sex? Sure—beats the hell out of algebra.

Having sex, though, was obviously not like doing math sums. By approaching it as coldly as any other subject, the curriculum managed to strip away all of its ethical context. So while we learned to rattle off the most effective forms of contraception as expertly as any prostitute (better, actually, since we memorized their failure rates), we never discussed—not even vaguely—under what circumstances we should consider sex right or wrong. We were certainly not taught, as girls, that our ability to conceive imposed any special, or extra, responsibility upon us beyond the technicalities of contraception. From the curriculum's viewpoint, men and women—if different in basic plumbing—shared essentially the same sexual desires and were entitled to pursue them and express them in similar ways. The prevailing wisdom then, as it is now, was that for too long children—particularly girls—had been kept ignorant of their bodies and taught to be ashamed of their sexual desire. If left to our allegedly prudish and/or ignorant parents, we might have been told not to have sex until we were older or, more unrealistically, until we were married. But an enlightened education system was one that understood the "reality" of teenage sexual behavior and tried to accommodate it rather than change it. They had not yet begun to hand out condoms or instruct students in how to unroll them over bananas, but the assumptions that led to these advances were all in place.

Of course, the schools' eagerness to liberate us sexually was just one of many influences upon us. But the sex education curriculum epitomized the sexual ideology that was overtaking *everybody*—including our otherwise stodgy teachers. Our educators' fear that our homes were insufficiently sexually enlightened was sweetly naïve. By then, most of us had avidly read the copies of *Our Bodies, Ourselves* and *The Sensuous Woman* that we'd come across on our parents' (or friends' parents') bookshelves. Many of my classmates came from divorced families, as I did myself, and some had been subjected to a parade of their parents' lovers through their homes. By age thirteen and fourteen, the more sexually developed boys and girls had already undergone crash courses in contraception in unsupervised rec rooms after school. By grade seven, I'd seen my first pregnant student: Far from being banished from the hallways as she would have been only a decade before, she proudly walked the halls with her swelling belly.

It should be said that this new, liberated attitude toward teen sex didn't actually make sex less embarrassing to a thirteen- or fourteen-year-old. Nor did it make one feel any less self-conscious about the development of one's body. But it contributed its bit to the annihilation of the qualms that once kept most middle-class females "good girls" until a ring was on their finger. The seemingly neutral, value-free sexual instruction we received was, of course, crammed with moral messages. When our health teachers told us to watch our cholesterol, it was because they expected us to eat, and when they warned us to "use protection," it was of course because they expected us to have sex. And their message was repeated in triplicate all around us: on television and in movies, in books and magazines, even in the little pamphlets issued by tampon companies that celebrated all the magnificent changes taking place in our bodies. As my friends and I grew into young women, our sexual experience may have varied, but our attitude toward sex did not. You had sex with someone or you didn't. You regretted it or you enjoyed it. You wanted to see him again or you never wanted to see him again. You sometimes used a man or felt used by him. But unless you were unusually religious, you did not think about sex as a privilege of marriage, or even of an especially devoted relationship. If you were attracted to a man and he was attracted to you, you expected to have sex with him as naturally as you expected a gray sky to rain or spring to follow winter: The only questions were when and how. Carelessly, thoughtlessly, casually, sex—in the short space of a single generation— went from being the culminating act of committed love to being a precondition, a tryout, for future emotional involvement. If any.

◆　◆　◆

TODAY, FEW would still advocate the heady, unbridled, anything-goes approach to sex that prevailed in the 1970s. The right to sleep with as many men as a woman pleases has turned out to be a rather hollow freedom—at least if a woman seeks more than a series of groping, bodily encounters with men with whom she shares little but compatible sex organs. Anatole France bitterly remarked, "The law, in its majestic impartiality, forbids both rich and poor to sleep under bridges." The woman who comes of age today quickly discovers that she enjoys a similar guarantee of sexual "equality": the right to make love to a man and never see him again; the right to be insulted and demeaned if she refuses a man's advances; the right to catch a sexually transmitted disease that might, as a bonus, leave her infertile; the right to an abortion when things go wrong, or, as it may be, the right to bear a child out of wedlock.

Indeed, in all the promises made to us about our ability to achieve freedom and independence as women, the promise of sexual emancipation may have been the most illusory. These days, certainly, it is the one most brutally learned. All the sexual bravado a girl may possess evaporates the first time a boy she truly cares for makes it clear that he has no further use for her after his own body has been satisfied. No amount of feminist posturing, no amount of reassurances that she doesn't need a guy like that anyway, can protect her from the pain and humiliation of those awful moments after he's gone, when she's alone and feeling not sexually empowered but discarded. It doesn't take most women long to figure out that sexual liberty is not the same thing as sexual equality.

"Do these experiences make women stronger, as the sexual liberationists asserted?" wondered writer Lisa Schiffren in a 1997 essay for *The Women's Quarterly.* "I doubt it. It can only weaken a young woman's confidence in herself, her judgment, and the society around her when she experiences the powerlessness of being dumped after sleeping with someone, when she was led to believe that she had just as much control over the events as the guy. For more than a generation now, that is how girls have learned the truth about their control of the powerful force of sex unbounded by formal commitment. Because when that happened, nothing, not waiting patiently, not calling with some hokey pretext, not taking matters into one's own hands and inviting him for dinner or whatever the geniuses at the women's magazines advised, would turn things around. The unfair, ugly fact about the mating dance is that so much of female sexual power depends upon withholding oneself. If anything, that is even truer in an age when all the other girls are available, too."

If sexual liberation had worked out for women the way it was supposed to, then by now we would be living in an age of unprecedented sexual harmony. Schoolgirls have been educated in sexual techniques with which, in an earlier day, they could have shocked a sailor. Female sexual independence is celebrated everywhere, whether it's by the gyrating rock star rubbing her crotch on MTV, or the predatory, half-naked models advertising perfume on the sides of public buses, or the sexually precocious teenagers in television shows like *Beverly Hills 90210,* or the articles in women's magazines that offer tips for fellatio as breezily as they do hints for applying lipstick ("A pleasant-tasting lubricant such as Astroglide facilitates any hand action," advised an article in the June 1997 issue of *Mademoiselle*).

Yet you could also argue that women have never been more publicly degraded or exploited than they are in these supposed tributes to our sexual emancipation—tributes composed, by the way, as much by women scriptwriters, editors, and advertising executives as by men. Is there anyone who really thinks it is progress, for instance, that women are now casually portrayed as heroin addicts and child prostitutes in fashion photos or that most people no longer blink at nearly bare breasts on magazine covers in the checkout lines of supermarkets? Do the editors of women's magazines really think their young female readers are emancipated by such knowledge as *Cosmopolitan* offered in its September 1997 issue: "Easy Orgasms—How to Make Them Mind-Blowing and a Lot Less Work"? I remember pushing my then two-year-old daughter in her stroller along Third Avenue in New York and passing a bus shelter displaying a large picture of a man having sex from behind with a woman he'd pushed up against a brick wall. It was an advertisement for jeans. What would *this* tell my daughter about all the gains made by women in society? I wondered. And how on earth was I supposed to explain it to her? "What's that lady doing, Mummy?" I imagined her asking me. "Oh, just getting buggered in an alleyway, dear. It's just one of the many sexual opportunities you'll be able to have when you're older, if you're lucky." Fortunately, I saw the ad before she did, and cut across the street.

That women may actually be the losers in the sexual revolution is an idea just dawning on this generation of young women, who feel as sexually free as it is possible to feel and yet are so often powerless to experience anything more with the opposite sex than unsatisfying, loveless flings. Boys—even nice boys at elite colleges—rarely ask girls out anymore, to a movie or for coffee. Instead, young people go to big parties or out with each other in large packs, drink, pair off, and, if the mood suits, have sex. "All the men want to do is hook up—and most of them don't bother to call in the morning," complained a female undergraduate at Georgetown University in an article for a campus publication about the sexual anarchy of college social life. Yet, "[all] these random hook-ups haven't added one iota of power to the average woman," she noted. "To be sure, there are a lot of girls who aren't bothered by the casual overnight scene. . . . But in the real world, the more casual that women allow their physical relationships with men to become, the less respect they earn. Men don't date us because they don't have to." "It was gross," a young female graduate of Princeton told me. "I had a boyfriend between my freshman and senior year, thank God, which saved me from having to participate in the dating scene. Even for formal dances, boys wouldn't bother to ask girls to go with them, and some girls would get desperate the few nights before the dance, not wanting to just 'show up' or arrive in a group, so they'd call and ask out the boys themselves. It was brutal."

A 1997 *New York* magazine cover story detailed the sordid sex lives of students at the city's affluent private schools. What was most fascinating about the world the article described, however, was not so much the eye-popping level of promiscuity but how old-fashioned the boys' reactions were to the girls who slept with them. Even among these decadent, cynical teenagers, a surprisingly familiar morality play was taking place. While the female students boasted like boys of their sexual experiences, they were aware that their reputations had been badly damaged and that the boys had lost respect for them. "Everybody knows who everybody's had sex with, and everything is reputation," acknowledged a female student from Columbia Prep. The boys learned quickly which girls were experts at giving sexual pleasure—"the queen of buffs"—and who'd slept with everyone—the "hos," "trocks," and "hoochies." The girls who continued to cling to their lovers offered sad and self-deluded excuses: "We're not just there [having sex with the gangs]. We have a *role*," insisted one. "They get really territorial about us," said another proudly. "They'd be nothing without us." In order to keep the boys' attention, the girls were reduced to being grateful caregivers—the women the men always come back to in the end, who fetch them drinks, who are there for them when they strike out at bars, who nurse them when they're sick and bandage their wounds, and even tidy up after them. This is not a deal, I think, of which the liberationists would be proud. "Who do you think babies [the boys] and holds their head over the toilet?" a girl named Alex told the *New York* reporter. "At the end of the night," said another girl, "if they've trashed somebody's house, the girls are like, 'We're sorry,' 'Thank you very much,' and we help clean up." That wasn't exactly how the boys saw it. "I treat 'em how I meet 'em," said a male student callously. "If you meet 'em and the girl's sucking my man's dick in the bathroom, then they're gonna get treated like that." The girls who sleep around "are not girlfriend material." Explained one, "You're not going to go *out* with a girl who's a shookie [slut]." Yet as one of the girls put it, in order to win the boys' attention and acceptance, "She has to be down and dirty. They have to see you not be a priss—be like a man, basically."

And there, in a sentence, is the catch-22 of sexual liberation—not just for the elite students of Manhattan private schools, but for all of us. The goal was for women to be as free as men to express their sexual desires, and as frequently, without consequence. But the truth is, of course, that there are consequences—and very predictable ones, of our grandmothers' I-told-you-so variety.

There's a crude Yiddish expression that sums up the ancient sexual bargain between men and women: "No *chuppy*, no *schtuppy*." It means, literally, "No marriage, no sex." There's that other cliché, too, muttered by disapproving mothers for generations: "Why buy the cow when she's giving away the milk for free?" We may smirk at its primness, but as women—even as liberated, sexually uninhibited women—we still know *exactly* what it means. Men and women, by the very nature of their biology, have different, and often opposing, sexual agendas. Eventually most women want children and, with them, a committed husband and father. Yet so long as there is no readily understood and accepted way for women to say no to men they like and hope to see again, women lose their power to demand commitment from men. In that sense, as women, we are all equal—in our powerlessness. The woman who holds back from sex, waiting for the right man to come along, will find that no right man does—because he can get what he needs elsewhere—just as the woman who gives herself freely discovers that she holds no firmer grasp over him, either. The sexual revolution, from a male point of view, could be summed up as, "You mean I get to do whatever I want—and then leave? Great!"

Our grandmothers might have led more sheltered sex lives, but they also controlled what amounted to a sexual cartel: setting a high price for sexual involvement and punishing both men and women if they broke the agreement (either by forcing them into marriage or by ostracizing them from respectable company). Sexual rules create sexual solidarity among women. If men feel that they can flit from woman to woman, they will. They will enjoy our ready availability and exploit it to their advantage. But if women *as a group* cease to be readily available—if they begin to demand commitment (and real commitment, as in marriage) in exchange for sex—market conditions will shift in favor of women.

This is, to put it mildly, an unfashionable idea. To modern women, particularly *young* modern women, the loss of sexual freedom may not seem worth it. And it would fly in the face of our sense of fairness. If men are not constrained, why should we be? Today, a woman's right to pursue sexual pleasure is regarded with the same sanctity as her right to free speech. An unhappy single woman may attempt to improve her life by giving up such things as chocolate, fatty foods, and men who treat her badly, but she would never *think* of surrendering her sexual liberty. That heady, impassioned moment when a woman allows herself to give in to her desires—when she *chooses* to sleep with a man—is as essential to her identity as a modern woman as putting on a suit and going out to work. Her sexual freedom is the expression—indeed the embodiment—of her independence. And in expressing it willfully, and upon whim, she can feel fully the equal of a man. Even the most politically conservative young women I know—women who say they oppose abortion and yearn to marry and have families—would never disavow their right to sleep with whomsoever they please.

Young women now strut about like female Don Juans, expressing pride in their sexual conquests and their ability to control men sexually. You see them lining the bars or screeching into the microphones of clubs in downtown Manhattan, dressed in their end-of-millennium miniskirts and vinyl brassieres, lips smudged brown and hair tousled, virtually daring men to become sexually entangled with them. Like modern Amazons, they recoil from the idea that they need a relationship with a man in order to define who they are or to give meaning to their lives.

Or do they? If women were really as powerful as they like to claim, why are they so angry? Diatribes against men, wrote Ann Powers in a special 1997 "girl issue" of the rock magazine *Spin*, "[spill] forth on the college-radio airwaves like flash floods, furious and shocking. The mood [is] one of vengeance, the same spirit cultivated by Susan Faludi's best-selling book *Backlash*, which detailed contemporary sexism in terms that called for a war against it. Young women took that directive to heart, publishing zines with titles like *Chainsaw* and forming defiantly dirty bands like '7 Year Bitch.' "

Rather than stemming from power, however, their anger more likely stems from frustration. And with good reason. Men *are* getting away with appalling behavior toward women. But we are letting them get away with it—and then, out of sexual pride, or pain, or embarrassment, refusing to admit it to ourselves. Unfortunately, anger doesn't work any better than easy availability does. The lead singer of a group called "riot grrl queens Bikini Kill" may shout such lyrics as "Suck my left one!" but ten years from now, she (or, at any rate, many of her fans) may wonder why no man bothers to answer back. It's not simply that as you grow older, the queue of men willing to play it your way grows shorter, just as the list of things you want from them—commitment, a home, family—grows longer. (Even a super-Amazon like Madonna, who built her career defying and mocking conventional female roles, decided in her thirties that she'd like to have a baby and settle down: "Ever since my daughter was born," she told *Rolling Stone*, "I feel the fleetingness of time.") It's that the very nature of these kinds of relationships grows boring—and coarsening. A 1996 survey by *Mademoiselle* detected a change of heart in its otherwise lustful twentysomething readers. More than three quarters of the 715 women who responded to the survey checked off boxes that said they'd had "sex with strangers," "sex with one-night stands," and "casual, meaningless flings"—but the majority (52 percent) admitted that they enjoyed sex most when they were in love and in a "committed" relationship. "You don't want to get embroiled if it's not going to pan out," burbled the copy announcing the results. "If there's no love, there's no point."

The question is, though, what does "pan out" mean these days? All the sexual power a woman imagines herself possessing at twenty or twenty-two may evaporate the moment she attempts to use it to make a man stick around a few years later. Even a beautiful woman's looks are not enough to hold a man forever; there are always more beautiful or younger or less demanding women coming along. And if a man does not feel like staying, there is none of the old social pressure upon him to do so.

A friend of mine, a very pretty woman in her early twenties, was at one point dating three men simultaneously, two of whom wanted to marry her. She said she and her friends chuckle at the occasional articles they read that suggest there is a shortage of marriageable men. How could there be a shortage, when every woman she knew was beating them off? But then she also acknowledged that these articles were usually written by women older than herself, who had been preoccupied with establishing themselves in their careers, who had felt strongly that they were "too young" to get married at her age, only to realize belatedly that very few thirty-five-year-old women have the sexual power over men that they had at twenty-five. And then my friend admitted that when she and her friends were not beating away their suitors, they were compulsively discussing what they were going to do with their lives. If they were too young to get married now, then *when?* And *whom* would they marry?

Their uncertainty about what it was, exactly, that they wanted to do pushed them into the quasi-serious but ultimately unsatisfying relationships that define (or, rather, in their ambiguity, fail to define) modern single life. These young women dated—meaning, they went out to dinner with—a number of men and got involved with—meaning, they slept with—a number of others, their involvements lasting three, maybe six, maybe eight months before fizzling out. Sometimes an infatuated couple would audition for marriage by deciding to live together. The exciting day of renting the U-Haul would arrive, and the two would merge the collected belongings of their single lives: his stereo and her sofa, his television and her frilly bedskirt, his coffee table and her potted palm. They made their first exhilarating trips to Pottery Barn and Crate & Barrel, choosing wineglasses and colorful plates with which to entertain their friends in their new life as Committed Couple. But the game of playing house together when it did not lead to marriage (as it often doesn't) led them to experience all the disadvantages of monogamy with few of its benefits. Sex lost its initial passion and novelty. They would find themselves engaged in petty arguments over who would tidy up and cook. And at the same time, they lacked the emotional glue that binds people who have, simply through the act of marrying, announced their intention to form a family and stick it out. Instead, they came to occupy the position of the old married couple in their social circle while their friends continued to live romantic, adventurous, single lives—or so it suddenly appeared to them. And because they had signed a lease on an apartment that neither could afford alone, they'd ensnared themselves. They stayed together long past the time that they would have had they never moved in with each other in the first place—sometimes as much as a year or two longer. And then they were overwhelmed by the bitter sense of wasted time.

So women find themselves in a bewildering position: They want the benefits of the old sexual deal (marriage and family), but they are unwilling to accept the sexual restraint that brought the old deal into existence. Instead, a young woman thinks that things will somehow simply fall together—that when *she* chooses to retire from the nightlife and settle down, there will be an ample selection of decent, solicitous men eagerly waiting to marry her. And then she may well grow angry at the behavior of the men she meets—men who like receiving *their* benefits from the new sexual deal (that is, sex) without having to pay the old price of commitment.

It is interesting that so many prime-time TV shows now feature *unglamorous*, single, thirtyish female characters neurotically brooding about their thwarted love lives. The sexually empowered woman as depicted by sexual revolutionaries like Germaine Greer and Erica Jong and popularized by schlock novelists like Judith Krantz in countless miniseries seems to have disappeared altogether from television. To the lonely urban woman, the times before the sexual revolution suddenly do not look so bad. When you're a single woman having no sex, or only very unsatisfying sex, it's hard not to envy those generations of women that lacked our sexual freedom but could at least expect straightforward, respectful, and romantic courtship leading to marriage. The desire to be pursued and courted, to have sex with someone you love as opposed to just barely know, to be certain of a man's affection and loyalty—these are deep female cravings that did not vanish with the sexual revolution.

Perhaps that explains the otherwise mysterious success of late-twentieth-century movies based on nineteenth-century novels of manners, such as *The Age of Innocence, Pride and Prejudice, Emma,* and *Sense and Sensibility.* What is striking about the modern film adaptions is their almost pornographic obsession with the vanished protocol of daily life: the constricting costumes that distinguished ladies and gentlemen from common folk; the engraved calling cards on silver trays; the elaborately choreographed minuets and waltzes; the stiff exchanges of bows and curtsies; and, above all, the excruciatingly polite restraint that governed every interaction between men and women, even passionate declarations of love. They are airbrushed, sentimental views of the past, to be sure, but it's the urge to airbrush that is the most arresting thing about them. It's hard to imagine that you could have made such films twenty years ago without underscoring the cold indifference of the upper classes toward the lower or the suppression of women. It's as if popular taste now wishes to recall the past only for its good points, and particularly that lost civility between men and women.

"Hard to imagine," wrote an astonished *New York Times* reporter in a 1996 lifestyle feature, "but being a debutante is back." The writer went on to describe the revival of this pageant of female modesty in all its de-tails—from the frothy, organza gowns to the male escorts dubbed Deb's Delights—that were once thought entirely killed off by feminism. The new debutantes, however, perfectly embodied the limits of modern nos-talgia. For as much as these silk-clad young women wished to reenact the balls of forty years ago, they would hardly wish to restore the function that these events once served. So, even as girls normally given to slouch-ing around their wealthy parents' apartments in jeans and untucked shirts effused to the *Times* over how much they loved to dress up and dance, they were ignorant of, or treated as a joke, the old purpose of these balls: to launch society's most prominent virgins directly into the arms of suitable husbands. Some of the new debutantes attended with their live-in boyfriends, and the organizer of the event acknowledged that marriage was the furthest thing from anyone's minds. "For this to be a marriage market now," she was quoted as saying, "we'd have to do this when the girls are in their thirties." The irony, though, is that it was precisely the strict sexual code that these young women reject, and not the fancy dresses, that gave these affairs their romantic *frisson,* infusing every word and gesture a man and woman exchanged with meaning. There is going to be a lot more sparkle and sexual tension if the stakes are, "Is this the man I'm going to marry?" than, "Will he sleep with me?" Minus the code, these rituals become little more than passing fashion, and sex itself merely the physical expression of passing affection.

I happened to watch the movie *Emma* with a thirty-two-year-old sin-gle woman friend of mine, who afterward exclaimed sorrowfully, "There are no Mr. Knightleys!" But if there are no more Mr. Knightleys, then it's because there are no more Emma Woodhouses, either. The two can only exist in a world in which each supports and reinforces the character of the other. Readers of the book *Emma* will recall the scene in which Knightley takes Emma to task for a careless remark that hurts the feelings of her spinster friend Miss Bates. As they return to the carriage, Knightley draws Emma aside to rebuke her for forgetting herself *for a moment:* "I cannot see you acting wrong without remonstrance," he tells her. "How could you be so unfeeling to Miss Bates? How could you be so insolent in your wit to a woman of her character, age, and situation?—Emma, I had not thought it possible." Emma is devastated by Knightley's criticism, and weeps all the way home. But she understands, too, the moral responsibility she must take for even the most trivial of her personal actions, which have consequences for those around her.

And this—not the settings of silverware—is what we modern women ought to take away from these old stories: the importance of agreed-upon standards of behavior. It is these above all else that we lost in the sexual revolution. These standards appear very musty to us now, like archaic codes of medieval chivalry. Men no longer stand when a woman enters a room. We don't expect men to let us enter or leave elevators first or to surrender their seats to us on the bus, even if we're pregnant. (When I was nine months' pregnant in New York City, the only people ever to offer their seats were elderly women, who couldn't fathom why no one else would stand up. The men, no matter how fit or burly, would resolutely stare right through my bulging stomach.) We got rid of those rules of etiquette because they drew sexual distinctions—distinctions that seemed odious because they presumed female weakness (hence the great 1970s feminist rebellion against men holding open doors for them: "I can open it *myself*"). That we may say good riddance to the strict rules of the past does not make it any easier to operate in a world in which there are very few rules at all. It is like trying to write without any rules of grammar or punctuation: Men and women have lost the grammar of courtship and love. Affairs are pursued or dropped; we mingle and move on. But there are no certainties, no "If I do A—or he does A—then that must lead to B." And women are hurt most of all by this absence of rules.

The elaborate rituals that used to govern relations between the sexes were based on the understanding that women, as child bearers, required the protection of society against men who might recklessly use and abandon them. These rituals could be inhibiting and stultifying, yes, but they at least did the job of letting everyone know what was appropriate and inappropriate behavior. And at best, they protected women from the potentially disastrous consequences of ungoverned male lust. Because these rituals were so relentlessly specific—whether it was in the rules about the wearing of gloves by ladies or hats by men—they sharpened and focused the sexual signals exchanged between the sexes. Once upon a time, a man could be pretty sure about the "sort of girl" who might be open to his advances merely by her appearance—she offered him clues in the cut of her dress, in her flirtatious manner. A woman who gave out no such signals had the right to slap a man if he presumed her to be *that* sort of girl. Today, men and women have no such ready ways of signaling each other. The woman in the gray pinstripe suit could well be the sort of girl angling for an affair with her male boss, while the punk rocker in torn net stockings, leather miniskirt, and lace bustier may be the kind to take offense at a passerby's whistle.

These little rules of daily life protected a larger sexual order, one that ushered men and women into marriage at a younger age and kept them there by clamping down on extramarital temptations. Women, much more than men, depend on each other to agree on the terms by which we conduct our sex lives. If women don't settle down at the same time as their friends, if we insist upon our right to lead sexually unconstrained lives into our thirties and beyond, then we have to accept that there will be consequences to the long-term stability of *all* marriages, and even to our own ability to marry. The twenty-two-year-old attractive woman, feeling as sexually powerful as it is possible to feel, will be unlikely to sympathize much with the thirty-three-year-old woman who complains about the shortage of men, just as she will have difficulty understanding a married woman's mistrust of her, except as a function of envy. A young woman will not readily see that her sexual actions have any bearing on the other women around her, and certainly not upon those older than herself. The truth is, however, that a young woman's actions *intimately* affect the lives of other women, even those she doesn't know. If young, attractive women offer no-strings-attached sex, then men will have no pressing reason to tie themselves down. This might be of little concern to a woman who is not yet ready to settle down, but sooner or later it will become of urgent concern.

I once spoke to a group of female college students at a conference in Washington, D.C. Their conversation quickly digressed into a discussion of their frustrating sex lives. They voiced the modern girl's lament, one that might be baldly expressed as: To put out or not to put out? They did not want to be thought prudish, nor did they want to be thought easy. If they restrained themselves, the men faded away, and if they gave in, the men faded away. So what to do?

It is a difficult question to answer, particularly if you reject, as these girls did, any implication that women have a *special* responsibility to restrain themselves from having sex. Women understandably tend to get squeamish whenever female sexual restraint is discussed, not least because throughout history they have been largely the ones to be punished, often severely, with scarlet letters, stonings, and burnings for sexual misconduct (let's not overlook the fact, though, that men have been horse-whipped, shunned, and shamed into deadly duels for *their* sexual misdemeanors). Yet even while the revival of the scarlet letter is hardly a possibility in daytime-talk-show America, we still speak about curbs on female sexual behavior as if *any* restraint at all on the part of women will automatically return us to Victorian levels of female modesty and perhaps even to chastity belts.

Indeed, this is exactly the metaphor that opponents of a bill used when the New Jersey legislature attempted in 1993 to require school sex education programs to advocate abstinence. "This bill not only pushes New Jersey back to the Victorian era, it hurls the state all the way back into the Middle Ages, when chastity belts were considered the effective method of preventing pregnancies," said one agitated legislator. The women's magazines in particular avoid speaking of sex in ways that might suggest they are advocating female sexual reticence even when, in fact, they are. The

June 1997 issue of *Glamour,* for example, published an article called "The Hot, Happy Sex Life of a Virgin" by a woman who declared that just because you wanted to abstain from sex didn't mean you had to be an old maid about it. To the contrary, she wrote, "I've been touched, kissed, prodded, rubbed, caressed, licked, nibbled—you name it. More times than I'd like to admit. I don't fit the image of virgin except for one salient fact: I've never had sexual intercourse."

Some feminists go so far as to maintain that the problem for women today is not that they are suffering from the fallout of the sexual revolution, but that they are *not uninhibited enough.* "Women learn—still—that any sexual 'past' can be read as promiscuity, and that the taint of promiscuity can lead to social or professional censure," Naomi Wolf wrote in her 1997 book, *Promiscuities: The Secret Struggle for Womanhood.* While the sexual revolution should be heralded as a victory for women, Wolf says, in that it led to legalized abortion, contraception, and more widespread information about female sexuality, "we still did not inherit a culture that valued and respected female desire."

"Desire, apparently, is still a dirty word to many young women," agrees Kate Fillion, author of the 1996 book, *Lip Service.* This isn't terribly surprising given that they learn defensive sexuality—how to say No, how to react to boys who want sex—but aren't taught to think of themselves as sexual agents. Consequently, many are confused by and ashamed of their own sexual stirrings, and don't have a clue about what it means to own their sexuality." Katie Roiphe resents the hysterical tenor that now accompanies educators' warnings to teenagers about the risk of catching sexually transmitted diseases and AIDS, comparing it in spirit to the warnings Catholic priests used to issue about masturbation causing blindness. In her 1997 book, *Last Night in Paradise: Sex and Morals at the Century's End,* she complains that such warnings are merely an attempt to revive old-fashioned morality in modern terms, replacing the fear of committing sin with the fear of catching a disease. And the effect of this fear is to deprive young women of the sexual pleasure women experienced at the outset of sexual liberation, to dampen their passion, to make them . . . uptight. Describing an entirely different group of New

York private school kids from those encountered by the *New York* reporter, Roiphe is dismayed by these teenagers' expressed determination to *avoid* sexual adventure: "'I just don't think sex is something you should just do with someone for the fun of it,' a tall, athletic blonde explains to me earnestly. . . . These girls sound more responsible than my friends and I did at that age, more likely to stay away from fleeting encounters with the first boys who smile at them during a freshman week at college. . . . Their plans, and even their fantasies, involve a newly responsible and appropriate exchange of affections that would make the mother character of any Jane Austen novel proud. Their priorities are in order. They're not about to rush into anything. They're pursuing love over 'hooking up,' real knowledge of a person over glimpses, and they're not about to lose their heads over a stranger." But this, in Roiphe's eyes, is not necessarily a wise way to behave. It crushes impetuosity and kills romance. It puts you on the path to becoming staid, passionless, middle-aged. "Something unappealing comes along with this new caution," she says. Too much sexual suppression is as bad as too little. "As alarming as any of the long-haired visionaries of the Sixties are the typical Americans emerging from the current articles in *Time* and *Newsweek* who stay home and rent videos, and eat fat-free ice cream, and use the Stairmaster 3.5 times a week at the gym, never have more than one drink, and never feel the rush of unexpected intimacy coursing, dark and heavenly, through their veins." Nor, either, the rush from unexpected pregnancy by a man who, in the earthy atmosphere of morning, is someone with whom you don't even wish to share a toothbrush.

These writers come to different conclusions about what should be done. Wolf and Fillion believe young women need even more sexual education than they receive now, an education that would teach them "to articulate their sexual desires" (Fillion) and appreciate the "slut" side of themselves (Wolf). Roiphe hopes some reasonable median will be found between sexual anarchy and abstinence, but is unable to suggest what this compromise might look like. But they all agree that the solution, whatever it is, will not lie in any form of traditional morality; nor will it accept any difference between male and female sexual behavior. To these women, sex must always be a decision between two free agents, unhampered by moral considerations. Sex should be seen as having no lasting consequences, and it must never, ever be subject to social norms. Like the girl rockers, we must "empower ourselves," lest we succumb to conservative forces that would push us back to the days when women were ignorant of their orgasms, husbands were dull and inconsiderate lovers, and girls were judged as either chaste or depraved. "Despite all the evidence that the gender gap in sexual behavior is narrowing, traditional stereotypes continue to be repackaged, recycled, and reinforced in best-sellers and box office hits, greeting cards and academic treatises, sitcoms, and everyday conversations," Fillion laments. "[Women] continue to subscribe to the tidal wave theory in which women are compelled to have sex by forces of nature they are powerless to control: romantic love and/or the male sex drive."

BUT HERE we come full circle, back to the failed ideology of my 1970s health classes with a nineties feminist spin. So long as we persist in pretending that our sexuality is essentially the same as men's, we will be unable to confront the very real problems that arise from our difference. In the realm of sex, modern women sometimes seem like reckless teenagers issuing dares while desperately hoping all the time that the dare will never be called. We do not really want—or at least very few of us want—to live in a world of unbridled sexual freedom. And since we will no longer tolerate the old informal restraints upon men and women, we have been obliged to substitute the formal constraints of law. In order to give women the illusion of sexual freedom, we've had to impose increasingly stiff legal controls and penalties upon the sexual behavior of men.

"Sexual harassment" and "violence against women" did not exist as political issues a generation ago, which is not to say that the sort of incidents they refer to didn't happen. But it is interesting that sexual complaints against men have become most widespread at a time when men and women have otherwise achieved equality on all other fronts. Barely a week goes by when the news does not carry some item that suggests men are suddenly stampeding wildly and inexplicably out of control, whether it's sex scandals in the military, or the class-action sexual harassment suits filed by female employees against huge corporations, or the release of alarming statistics by women's organizations that purport to show that a woman is battered "every four minutes." A reasonable person could easily conclude that female soldiers are constantly being raped and threatened by their superiors, that huge numbers of bosses are groping unsuspecting female workers, that women risk grave physical injury when they enter into romantic relationships with seemingly normal men.

Feminists have used these incidents as evidence of a male "backlash" against women's equality. The more progress women make, the more resentful men become, and the more determined they are to knock us back into place. "The truth is," writes Susan Faludi, who introduced the theory in her 1991 book, *Backlash: The Undeclared War on American Women,* "the last decade has seen a powerful counter-assault on women's rights, a backlash, an attempt to retract the handful of small and hard-won victories that the feminist movement did manage to win for women." It is only by ever more draconian punishment for sexist behavior, feminists believe, that women can continue to progress. For this reason, feminist organizations have been eager to promote statistics that fan female mistrust and hostility toward men, even when the figures are untrue. Many of the claims issued by prominent feminist groups like the Battered Women's Justice Project and the National Coalition Against Domestic Violence, for example, are grossly exaggerated or false and often obviously so. The truth is that the number of sexual assaults against women has actually been *falling* in recent years, according to the National Crime Victimization Survey issued by the Bureau of Justice Statistics (between 1991 and 1996, the number of women raped per thousand dropped starkly from a rate of 2.24 to 0.90). Federal crime statistics show that men are more likely than women to be victims of violent crime both by acquaintances and by strangers. Married women are far less likely to be attacked than unmarried or separated or divorced women (the rate of attacks upon separated women is twenty-five times higher than that upon married women). There was never a shred of evidence that battery rose on Super Bowl Sunday, as the feminist groups claimed. (*Washington Post* reporter Ken Ringle attempted to trace this story to its source and was never able to find one, or find any increased incidence of battered women calling police departments and shelters on that day when crime traditionally goes *down*.)

Still, there's no doubt that many men physically hurt women—nothing new about that, or about the rape and assault laws that have for centuries punished such crimes. What is new is the phenomenon of women turning to judges and human rights commissions to discipline very mild cases of male aggression—that so many women no longer feel able to protect themselves against even irritating remarks by men. Nowhere is this more apparent than in the workplace. Since the Anita Hill–Clarence Thomas hearings in 1991, there has been a staggering increase in the number of charges brought against men by female employees who are angered or feel injured by a sexual advance: Sexual harassment complaints filed with the Equal Employment Opportunity Commission, the federal agency that reviews these cases, jumped from 3,661 in 1981 to 14,420 in 1994, an increase of nearly 400 percent (in the year following the Hill-Thomas hearings, there was a startling 62 percent increase in the number of complaints). Yet what is remarkable about so many of these complaints—especially those that have resulted in the most sensational, multimillion-dollar court settlements—is not the seriousness of the male behavior being punished but its mildness. A woman no longer needs to show that her refusal of a man's advances caused her to lose her job or stymied her promotion in a firm, merely that his actions caused her discomfort. In 1995, a court awarded $50 million to a female clerk in the receiving department of Wal-Mart whose supervisor joked about her figure; in 1994, a secretary received $3.5 million—including $50,000 for emotional distress—for enduring a few clumsy passes from her boss, a patent attorney (who was subsequently fired for professional misconduct). Compare that to what is considered the first ever sexual harassment lawsuit: In 1974, a female employee at the Environmental Protection Agency said she'd been fired for refusing to have an affair with her boss. She won the case, but only on appeal, and received $18,000 in back pay as damages.

Some of us had a hard time sympathizing with Anita Hill because even if everything she said was true, Thomas' actions hardly amounted to harassment. By Hill's account, the most Thomas was guilty of was making a couple of off-color remarks and persistently inviting her to dinner. Thomas' alleged behavior did not prevent Hill from following him to a new job, or from seeking his recommendation for another, or from phoning him and keeping up her friendship with him a decade after they'd gone their separate ways. Furthermore, at no point did she feel compelled to say anything to him *personally* about the behavior that she later insisted had caused her so much distress; her charges, from his point of view, came as a bolt from the blue. Which leaves one to wonder, what sort of state of affairs have we arrived at when a woman feels no obligation to warn a man directly that something he does bothers her, but is prepared to humiliate him and attempt to destroy his career a decade later?

Hill's accusations set the stage for the lawsuit of Paula Jones against President Clinton. While feminists took a vocal stand in every previous high-profile sexual harassment case—whether it was Senator Bob Packwood, who was forced to resign, or the military officers in the Tailhook and Aberdeen incidents (who received prison sentences of up to twenty-five years for having consensual sex with subordinates), or the assembly-line workers in the massive $34 million lawsuit against Mitsubishi Motors—they went silent when the presidential scandal erupted in early 1998. Gloria Steinem strongly defended the president's relationship with then twenty-one-year-old White House intern Monica Lewinsky by arguing it was consensual, but this was an astonishing defense for Steinem to make. The previous feminist definition of sexual harassment—one the U.S. military and many corporations now accept—is that because of the power disparity, sex between a male superior and female subordinate can never be truly consensual. And even if Steinem had suddenly decided to dissent from that expansive definition of harassment, it was still hard to understand how any person who considers herself "pro-woman" could defend adultery—after all, had the president's wife given her consent to this behavior?—or condone the highest executive in the land treating a young female staff member like his personal geisha. By contrast, when Senator Packwood resigned, NOW president Patricia Ireland said, "They [the senators] understand that their constituents will no longer tolerate the abuse of power or the abuse of women by those in power." She added, "Packwood has shown such great disrespect for the law and for women, he should not be allowed to lead the charge in changing laws that impact women." But with Anita Hill, these same feminists had opened a Pandora's box, and it was too late to regret it when they saw it consuming one of their own political favorites.

Unfortunately, the box remains open, and the chilling and vindictive sexual atmosphere that has resulted is not one that most of us would have chosen as the outcome of the push for sexual equality. Corporations have reacted to the post–Anita Hill climate by implementing more and more elaborate policies governing the most trivial exchanges between men and women. It is now common—and in some states required by law of corporations of a certain size—for companies to offer sexual harassment awareness and prevention programs to their employees, to provide manuals and display posters warning against sexual harassment, and to hire professional consultants to evaluate their efforts just in case the company has overlooked some form of behavior that might conceivably be misconstrued as a sexual advance. One consultant told me that she warned her male executive clients never to close their office doors when meeting with a female employee. They are likewise urged to avoid making any remarks of a personal nature, such as "That shirt is a pretty color for you" or "Did you change your hair? It looks nice." Male employees are reluctant to take business trips with female colleagues or to be alone with them, out of fear of spurious charges. The same goes for all physical contact, lest that triumphant pat-on-the-back-for-work-well-done ends up costing a man—as it did the bewildered owner of a California computer company—$100,000 to settle a lawsuit.

It's possible to dismiss these cases as the more ridiculous examples of an overly litigious society in which there are lucrative incentives to sue: Why not haul your boss to court if there is a good chance his unwitting compliment and reckless wink could make you rich? But I think these cases reflect something worse than ordinary lawsuit mania. They suggest that men and women can no longer be trusted to work out even their most mundane sexual disagreements privately. This isn't to say that genuine sexual harassment doesn't occur and that it shouldn't be punished when it does. But when women are taking men to court for an unwanted compliment, something has truly broken down in the sexes' ability to deal with each other. Writer Carolyn Graglia observes, "Today, well-educated, professional women, who are embarrassed to defend the unsophisticated concepts of virginity and chastity, are less competent to control men's sexual advances than high school girls in the 1940s." If women no longer enjoy ready protection from men who "cross the line," it is because most lines have been erased—except legal ones. We now must turn to the courts to redefine the limits that were once observed socially and ask judges to level the face slap we once could confidently administer ourselves.

The trouble with asking the law to step in and monitor our sexual relations, however, should be obvious and disturbing. The law cannot begin to cope with the subtleties of romantic disagreements. It likes its cases clear-cut, its wrongdoing blatant. With the exception of a few straightforward criminal acts—rape and assault—disputes arising from love and sex are notoriously messy. They can't be wrapped up neatly like a parking violation or a mugging. As the Hill-Thomas hearings vividly illustrated, so much of the wronged party's complaint can rest upon the possible misinterpretation of a remark or the misreading of a gesture. Then there are all the deep, personal motives a judge cannot know: Is a woman using the law to exact revenge upon a man who once scorned *her* advances? Might there be some complicated history between them that would be better worked out in the presence of a psychologist than a circuit court justice? Rarely are there objective witnesses—or, for that matter, any witnesses at all—to crimes of the heart (Hill could not produce one). Ultimately, they boil down to her word versus his.

Worse, over recent years, the definitions of what constitutes sexual harassment have become increasingly subjective, based upon how a woman *feels* about any given incident. Wholly new charges like "date rape" have been devised, in which there may have been no actual crime committed but the woman is left feeling as abused as if there had been. She decides that she was too drunk to have given her consent to sex and that the man with whom she'd been flirting took advantage of her—if it wasn't rape, it was *like* rape. She felt a male colleague's compliment of her skirt showed disrespect, and that he did not simply regard her as a fellow professional like himself—if it wasn't sexual harassment, it was *like* sexual harassment. I sometimes wonder whether Paula Jones would have sued the president if he'd offered her a glass of champagne and flirted a little with her before he (allegedly) lowered his pants; would she still have been affronted? (As one of my friends remarked, Jones might have been that kind of girl, just not *that* kind of girl.) Or look again at the feminist reaction to the Lewinsky matter. What if Lewinsky, instead of going quietly to the Pentagon (where she was transferred to after her involvement with the president), decided she was angry about it? Would she now have a sexual harassment case against the president, even though the sex she was having previously was seen, by both parties, as "consensual"?

This is where relying too heavily upon the law to broker our sexual disagreements ultimately fails. No matter how much we refine it to deal with every possible romantic circumstance, we will never be capable of eliminating the ineradicable differences—and thus opportunities for conflict—between the sexes. And that is not only because men and women are not sexually identical, but also because there are many other occasions when we *wish* to be treated differently, and the law can never know *which* occasions those are. In this sense, the controversy that has arisen over sexual issues in the courts merely reflects the confusion of the female population as a whole. Not just in court but in life, there is no general agreement about when we want to be treated like women—wooed, romanced, complimented, our femininity appreciated—and when we wish to be treated exactly as equals.

You see this most starkly in the military, where women have demanded the right to train and fight alongside the men just as long as they also retain the right to be treated like women when it suits them. They want to be given the same assignments in combat or on ships—even if they can't do the same number of push-ups as the average male soldier, or lift the same amount of weight, or even throw a grenade the distance required to avoid blowing themselves up. They want to fly the same missions—even if, as one female helicopter pilot in Panama expected, those missions have to be scheduled around the breast-feeding of an infant. A 1992 study on sexual harassment in the military by the General Accounting Office found that the majority of complaints women filed are over comments made by men about the double standards that exist for female soldiers (in other words, muttering that women can't physically keep up now constitutes sexual harassment). Similarly, a RAND study found that women considered it "harassment" when men grouped together to watch a movie—and not a porno movie, but simply an action film that the women weren't interested in watching. The military brass—like corporate executives— have leveled stricter and stricter codes governing the conduct of males, going so far as to order that they should not swear or say anything that might be construed as a sexual, or even uncomplimentary, remark toward women. The outcome is an incongruous set of rules that at once accepts women as fit for war and also treats them as creatures of such exquisite sensitivity that they will fall to pieces at a soldier's idle cuss.

WHICH WAY will we have it? To be treated exactly the same as men or differently from them?

That most women will reply "neither" or "somewhere in between" won't solve the problem. This is especially true for young women trying to navigate their way to marriage. The rules controlling sexual behavior used to be most rigorously applied to girls under the age of twenty-one because adults feared the volatile combination of raging hormones and emotional immaturity. If most girls did not attend debutante balls, they were subject to other elaborate rituals—chaperoned parties and dances, dates with boys scrutinized and approved by their parents, and the rather hasty fashion with which they married after that. Almost all the adults in a young woman's life conspired, whether she liked it or not, to protect her from predatory male sexual advances and romantic recklessness. Today, in our eagerness to abandon this constrained existence, we've made it almost impossible for teenagers to *avoid* having sex before the age of eighteen. The ideal of sexual freedom is now so zealously adhered to that many universities no longer maintain separate dormitories and bathrooms for men and women. A woman may notice a pair of hairy feet in the toilet stall next to hers or emerge from a shower in a towel only to bump into a man waiting to come in. If young men and women are going to bathe together, eat together, and study together, we can fully expect that they will sleep together. And of course they do. If a previous generation of women attended college primarily to find suitable husbands (or to get their M.R.S., as the joke went), young women arrive on campus today as much expecting to explore their sexual independence as furthering their knowledge of history and literature.

As I said before, all of this might be cause for celebration—evidence of our modern sexual enlightenment—if sexual liberation had turned out the way it was supposed to, with men and women sleeping together as often as they wish, serenely and without consequence. But its failure is perfectly demonstrated in these academic petri dishes, where sexual egalitarianism has been taken to its natural extreme and feminist reaction against men is at its most vehement and hysterical. On campuses across the country, scores of female students join in the annual "Take Back the Night March" to protest the alleged pervasiveness of male sexual violence. It's now customary at these demonstrations for women to stand before microphones and describe not only egregious acts of male abusiveness but the details of their sexual humiliations—the time a man interpreted a miniskirt and flirtatious manner as a come-on; the regret one felt for having drunken sex with a frat boy. In the telling, these incidents are given the same moral weight as rape. A woman is not expected to accept responsibility for actions that might have misled or confused the man; the man is always at fault, no matter how provocative the woman's manner or dress. In the new feminist understanding of male sexuality, a man must be punished for merely his *hope* of having sex with a woman. As for women, a friend of mine likes to joke, they no longer demand the right to free sex but to *good* sex. A casual fling that a woman finds pleasurable is not considered date rape. But the woman who wakes up the next morning feeling a little tawdry, wondering *what* it was that possessed her to have sex with *him*, may decide it wasn't her fault after all; somehow she must have been bullied into it.

Quite naturally, some young women have stepped forward to protest this chilling view of sex; like the writers Katie Roiphe, Karen Lehrman, and Rene Denfield, they compare the new feminists to prudish Victorians who regard women as frail flowers, helpless in the clutches of amorous men. *"We're not victims!"* they declare. And so they're not—at least not of what they think. For it's one thing to insist that women are perfectly capable of saying yes or no to sex and that they should be held just as responsible for their actions as men (bravo). It's another to pretend, as these women do, that women face no innate disadvantages in a world of sexual license. At least the radical feminists, in their crazed way, understand that female sexual freedom flourishes only if male sexual freedom is severely curbed. If women are going to have the "right" to dress and behave as they please, the "right" to be "sluts," then we shall have to crack down on the inevitable male reaction. For men have not suddenly become more beastly, as the hysterics would have us believe. Rather, they are responding to our behavior in a wholly predictable way. The woman who puts on a short skirt, teases her hair, gets tipsy, and with every gesture signals her sexual availability should not be surprised at the end of the evening that the man does in fact expect sex. Nor should she be surprised when, after lustily falling into bed with a man before she's even certain of his last name, he seems startled that she expects more of him than a one-night stand. What *should* surprise her is that there is no longer any social disapproval of this behavior. The feminists who prowl college campuses detecting harassment in a football player's leer may be unwilling to acknowledge female sexual responsibility, as their critics say; but they are also reacting to the consequences of a liberty that did not work out for women as its apostles hoped.

Still, to question whether the sexual revolution actually improved women's lives or harmed them seems a pointlessly old-fashioned exercise, like debating whether starving or feeding is best for treating colds. In reconsidering all the ways in which women's lives and attitudes have changed in a generation, very few critics would be willing to say that women's sexual liberation has been an altogether bad thing.

And how could they? As my friend and I walked from the movie theater that evening after watching *Emma,* I wondered if we could ever persuade women like us to don the late-twentieth-century equivalent of a corset and restrain their sex lives in order to promote marriage and monogamy. It would seem absurd to tell women—who are seeking graduate degrees, going to the office, living on their own—that they should have to wait for marriage to have sex; it would be akin to treating them like those young WWII GIs, who were seen as old enough to die for their country but not to take a sip of whiskey. And it would seem especially absurd to abstain if a woman is not even planning to get married until she is in her late twenties or early thirties. She may well wonder, Why bother?

But there is good reason to bother. If women do, by and large, wish to reunite sex with love, to regain male commitment, and to restore trust and civility between men and women—the most appealing aspects of traditional morality—then we are going to have to be prepared to put up with some of its restrictions, too. Instead of embracing the "slut within us," as Naomi Wolf advises, we should reject her, just as we should reject men who use and discard women.

Of course, we may continue to do as we do now and pretend that women are every bit as sexually free and nonchalant as men. But if we do wish to carry on with this pretense, then we should not express astonishment or resentment when men behave more badly than they used to, or show less inclination to stay with us, or that sex generally feels more meaningless. After all, when something becomes widely and cheaply available, its value usually goes down too.

Acknowledging sexual difference, however, does not require us to accept the hostile, invidious feminist view either—that men are innately violent and lustful while women are always blameless. It does not require us to see ourselves as victims, as weaker than or inferior to men. The new understanding of sexual differences might simply be found in the old understanding if we were willing to restore it and polish it up a bit. That understanding recognized the unique and often mysterious traits we instinctively think of as masculine and feminine, traits that have persisted despite all the ideological sandblasting of the past three decades. They are too subtle and elusive to be inscribed in law. They confound both poets and social scientists. But they are differences that complement each other—that ignite passion and sexual attraction, give love its depth and emotional sustenance, and ultimately form women into mothers and wives and men into fathers and husbands.

By denying these differences, we prolong the period when we are sexually vulnerable; we waste the opportunity in our passionate youth to find lasting love and everything that goes with it—home, children, stability, and the pleasure of sex as an expression of profound, romantic, and monogamous love. We have traded all this away for an illusion of sexual power and, in doing so, have abandoned the customs that used to protect and civilize both sexes, that constrained men and women but also obliged them to live up to their best natures. We might now be more free. But we enjoy less happiness, less fulfillment, less dignity, and, of all things, less romance.

chapter two

About Love

OUR GRANDMOTHERS, we are told, took husbands the way we might choose our first apartment. There was a scheduled viewing, a quick turn about the interior, a glance inside the closets, a nervous intake of breath as one read the terms of the lease, and then the signing—or not. You either felt a man's charms right away or you didn't. If you didn't, you entertained a few more prospects until you found one who better suited you. If you loved him, really *loved* him, all the better. But you also expected to make compromises: The view may not be great, but it's sunny and spacious (translation: he's not that handsome, but he's sweet-natured and will be a good provider). Whether you accepted or rejected him, however, you didn't dawdle. My late mother-in-law, who married at twenty, told me that in her college circles in the mid-1950s, a man who took a woman out for more than three dates without intending marriage was considered a cad. Today, the man who considered marriage so rashly would be thought a fool. Likewise, a woman.

Instead, like lords and sailors of yore, a young woman is encouraged to embark upon the world, seek her fortune and sow her oats, and only much later—closer to thirty than twenty—consider the possibility of settling down. Even religious conservatives, who disapprove of sex outside of marriage, accept the now-common wisdom that it is better to put off marriage than do it too early. The popular radio host Laura Schlessinger, traditional in so many of her views, constantly tells her listeners not to consider going to the altar before thirty. In 1965, nearly 90 percent of women aged twenty-five to twenty-nine were married; by 1996, only 56 percent of women in this age group were, according to the Population Reference Bureau in its 1996 survey, "The United States at Mid-Decade." Indeed, the more educated and ambitious a woman is the more likely she is to delay marriage and children, the Census Bureau reports. And if she doesn't—if such a young woman decides to get married, say, before she is twenty-five—she risks being regarded by her friends as a tragic figure, spoken of the way wartime generations once mourned the young men killed in battle: "How unfortunate, with all that promise, to be cut down so early in life!"

I remember congratulating a young woman upon her recent marriage to a friend of mine and commenting perfunctorily that both of them must be very happy. She was twenty-four at the time. She grabbed my hand, held it, and said with emotion, "*Thank you!*" As it turned out, I'd been the only woman to offer her congratulations without immediately expressing worry that she'd done the wrong thing. Her single female friends had greeted her wedding announcement as a kind of betrayal. A few had managed to stammer some grudging best wishes. Her best friend nearly refused to be a bridesmaid. They simply couldn't fathom why she'd tossed away her freedom when she was barely out of college. And she, in turn, couldn't convince them that she really *had* met the man she wanted to marry, that she didn't want to keep going out to bars in the evenings and clubs on the weekends, postponing her marriage for half a decade until she reached an age that her friends would consider more suitable.

In this sense, we lead lives that are exactly the inverse of our grandmothers'. If previous generations of women were raised to believe that they could only realize themselves within the roles of wife and mother, now the opposite is thought true: It's only *outside* these roles that we are able to realize our full potential and worth as human beings. A twenty-year-old bride is considered as pitiable as a thirty-year-old spinster used to be. Once a husband and children were thought to be essential to a woman's identity, the sources of purpose in her life; today, they are seen as peripherals, accessories that we attach only after our full identities are up and running. And how are we supposed to create these identities? They are to be forged by ourselves, through experience and work and "trial" relationships. The more experience we have, the more we accomplish independently, the stronger we expect our character to grow. Not until we've reached full maturity—toward the close of our third decade of life—is it considered safe for a woman to take on the added responsibilities of marriage and family without having to pay the price her grandmother did for domestic security, by surrendering her dreams to soap powders, screaming infants, and frying pans.

The modern approach to romance was perfectly captured in an item I came across one week in the wedding announcements of *The New York Times*. It was a short, lively description of a ceremony that had taken place between a twenty-eight-year-old graphic designer and a thirty-two-year-old groom. "I'm fiercely independent," the bride told the *Times* reporter. "My mother always told me, 'You don't need a man in your life. If you believe you need a man, you won't pursue your own goals.'" And pursuing her own goals is what the woman had done in the five years since meeting her future husband at a party in Portland, Oregon, where both had grown up. The bride, who looked like "a sturdier version of Audrey Hepburn," according to the *Times*, "slim enough to wear cigarette pants, but [also] as if she could change a tire or chop wood," dated but finally broke up with the man in order to move to Manhattan by herself. She said, "I never stopped loving [him], but we were doing our own separate things. Sometimes I think you have to do that in a relationship. It's easy to get complacent and not put yourself first." The man, who couldn't stop thinking about the woman, quit his job and followed her to New York a year later. Eventually they were engaged. As the *Times* noted, "While some couples see their wedding as the moment when everything from their bank accounts to their taste in food must merge," the bride would have none of it. "I think our independence has made us closer, because we both bring something to the relationship," she said. "D. H. Lawrence writes about two people in a relationship being like two stars who rotate around each other, attracted by each other's energy, but not dependent on each other." Their wedding took place, appropriately enough, on July Fourth.

But there is a price to be paid for postponing commitment, too, one this wedding announcement hints at. It is a price that is rarely stated honestly, not the least because the women who are paying it don't realize how onerous it will be until it's too late. The bride (whose photograph does show her to be nearly as pretty as a young Audrey Hepburn) embodies the virtues of a modern-day heroine: She is evidently free-spirited, self-confident, and determined to live, as Virginia Woolf exhorted, "an invigorating life" unimpeded by men. But she is lucky, too. For in order for this bride to realize her independence, she must remain so constantly self-centered that even when deeply in love, she cannot risk, as she puts it, becoming "complacent" and forgetting to put herself first. What if she hadn't found a suitor so willing to accommodate her quest? The groom isn't quoted in the article but is described by his friends as being "remarkably sweet-tempered." He would have to be! While he demonstrated that he was willing to quit his job and move to a new city just for the *chance* of being with her, she announced—to *The New York Times*, no less—that she wasn't prepared to make any such sacrifice on his behalf.

Of course, her attitude doesn't have to be read this way. And it usually isn't. How often have you watched a TV show or seen a movie or read a novel in which a woman is celebrated for finding the courage "to be herself" by leaving a marriage or starting a new career or telling a boorish husband he'll have to make his own dinner from now on? Her actions are not seen as selfish—or when they are, her selfishness is seen as payback for all the centuries of women's selflessness and sacrifice to men. Almost anything she does in the name of her own salvation and independence is justifiable. This rebellious model of womanhood, or the Selfish Heroine, as she might be called, began appearing in first-person magazine stories in the early 1970s and has been upheld by a generation of feminist writers and thinkers since. Virtually hundreds of novels and television movies-of-the-week have recycled the same plot. The story usually begins with an ending—the ending of a marriage. We meet a woman who is thwarted and depressed in her life as mother and wife. We then follow this woman's gradual enlightenment—her "journey of self-discovery"—as she comes to realize that true happiness lies in learning to value and love herself. She will begin putting her own needs first, until her old self is shed, and she blossoms into an entrepreneur or a congresswoman or maybe (if it's TV) a private detective. Newly confident, she'll trade in her insensitive, staid husband for an artistic and sensitive lover—a college professor or, possibly, a sculptor. Or she'll simply strike out on her own— with her kids or without them—to live a fuller, richer, and autonomous life peacefully by the seaside or in a funky downtown loft, surrounded by her own possessions. The modern fairy tale ending is the reverse of the traditional one: A woman does not wait for Prince Charming to bring her happiness; she lives happily ever after only by refusing to wait for him— or by actually rejecting him. It is those who persist in hoping for a Prince Charming who are setting themselves up for disillusionment and unhappiness.

"[I]t is a novel in which the narrator grabs us by the arm and hauls us up and down the block, to one home after another, and demands that we see for ourselves the ways in which, over and over, suburban housewives of the fifties and sixties came to live out a half-life," writes Susan Faludi in an afterword to a reissued edition of *The Women's Room*, Marilyn French's best-selling 1977 novel. "I had hoped for signs of outmodedness, but the same damn problems French identifies are still with us. . . ." You don't have to subscribe to Faludi's or French's hard-core feminist ideas to have absorbed their certainty that domesticity remains a threat to women's happiness. The idea that dependency is dangerous for women, that if we don't watch out for ourselves we risk being subsumed by men and family, that lasting happiness cannot be found in love or marriage— these are sentiments that are not considered at all radical and with which many more moderate women would agree. And while it's impossible to chart these things, I suspect it's this fear of dependency—more even than fear of divorce—that is primarily responsible for young women's tendency to delay marriage and childbirth.

Well, why not? Why should we tie ourselves down too young or believe that our only hope for happiness rests in finding lasting love? As we read in *The New York Times* of the groom who makes all the accommodations to the woman's plans, we may think, Bravo for her. Bravo for staying true to herself. This is progress. I remember having, in my early twenties, long and passionate conversations with my female friends about our need to be strong, to stand alone, to retain our independence and never compromise our souls by succumbing to domesticity. And yet at the same time, we constantly felt the need to shore each other up. We'd come across passages in books—paeans to the autonomy of the individual, replete with metaphors of lighthouses, mountains, the sea, etc.—copy them out carefully (in purple ink, on arty cards), and mail them to each other. It was as if despite our passion for independence, despite our confidence in ourselves as independent women, we somehow feared that even a gentle gust of wind blowing from the opposite direction would send us spiraling back into the 1950s, a decade none of us had experienced firsthand but one that could induce shudders all the same. Our skittishness is all the more surprising given that most of my friends' mothers, as well as my own, worked at interesting jobs and had absorbed as deeply as we had the cultural messages of the time. When I look back upon it, I think our youthful yearning to fall in love must have been enormously strong and at war with our equally fierce determination to stay free. We were fighting as much a battle against ourselves as against the snares of domesticity. And if one of us were to give way, the rest would feel weakened in our own inner struggles, betrayed by our friend's abandonment of the supposedly happy, autonomous life. For the truth is, once you have ceased being single, you suddenly discover that all that energy you spent propelling yourself toward an independent existence was only going to be useful if you were planning to spend the rest of your life as a nun or a philosopher on a mountaintop or maybe a Hollywood-style adventuress, who winds up staring into her empty bourbon glass forty years later wondering if it was all damn worth it. In preparation for a life spent with someone else, however, it was not going to be helpful.

　　And this is the revelation that greets the woman who has made almost a religion out of her personal autonomy. She finds out, on the cusp of thirty, that independence is not all it's cracked up to be. "Seen from the outside, my life is the model of modern female independence," wrote Katie Roiphe in a 1997 article for *Esquire* entitled "The Independent Woman (and Other Lies)." "I live alone, pay my own bills, and fix my stereo when it breaks down. But it sometimes seems like my independence is in part an elaborately constructed facade that hides a more traditional feminine desire to be protected and provided for. I admitted this once to my mother, an ardent seventies feminist . . . and she was shocked. I saw it on her face: *How could a daughter of mine say something like this?* I rushed to reassure her that I wouldn't dream of giving up my career, and it's true that I wouldn't." Roiphe then goes on to puzzle over how a modern woman like herself could wish for a man upon whom she could depend. "It may be one of the bad jokes that history occasionally plays on us," she concluded, "that the independence my mother's generation wanted so much for their daughters was something we could not entirely appreciate or want."

Unfortunately, this is a bit of wisdom that almost always arrives too late. The drawbacks of the independent life, which dawned upon Roiphe in her late twenties, are not so readily apparent to a woman in her early twenties. And how can they be? When a woman is young and reasonably attractive, men will pass through her life with the regularity of subway trains; even when the platform is empty, she'll expect another to be coming along soon. No woman in her right mind would want to commit herself to marriage so early. Time stretches luxuriously out before her. Her body is still silent on the question of children. She'll be aware, too, of the risk of divorce today, and may tell herself how important it is to be exposed to a wide variety of men before deciding upon just one. When dating a man, she'll be constantly alert to the possibilities of others. Even if she falls in love with someone, she may ultimately put him off because she feels just "too young" for anything "serious." Mentally, she has postponed all these critical questions to some arbitrary, older age.

But if a woman remains single until her age creeps up past thirty, she may find herself tapping at her watch and staring down the now mysteriously empty tunnel, wondering if there hasn't been a derailment or accident somewhere along the line. When a train does finally pull in, it is filled with misfits and crazy men—like a New York City subway car after hours: immature, elusive Peter Pans who won't commit themselves to a second cup of coffee, let alone a second date; neurotic bachelors with strange habits; sexual predators who hit on every woman they meet; newly divorced men taking pleasure wherever they can; embittered, scorned men who still feel vengeful toward their last girlfriend; men who are too preoccupied with their careers to think about anyone else from one week to the next; men who are simply too weak, or odd, to have attracted any other woman's interest. The sensible, decent, not-bad-looking men a woman rejected at twenty-four because she wasn't ready to settle down all seem to have gotten off at other stations.

Or, as it may be, a woman might find herself caught in a relationship that doesn't seem to be going anywhere or living with a man she doesn't want to marry. Or if she does want to marry the man she lives with, she may find herself in the opposite situation from the woman in *The New York Times:* Maybe the man she loves has taken at face value her insistence that nothing is more important to her than her independence. He's utterly bewildered by—or resentful of—her sudden demand for a wedding. Hasn't *she* always said a piece of paper shouldn't matter between two people who love each other? And because they are now living a quasi-married existence, she has no power to pressure him into marriage except by moving out—which will be messy and difficult, and might backfire. Whatever her circumstances, the single woman will suddenly feel trapped—trapped by her own past words and actions—at the moment other desires begin to thrust themselves upon her.

So much has been written about a woman's "biological clock" that it has become a joke of television sitcoms: career women who, without warning, wake up one morning after thirty with alarm bells ringing in their wombs. Actually, the urge for children and everything that goes with them—not just a husband, but also a home and family life—often comes on so gradually that it's at first easily brushed away. What a woman is aware of, at around the age of twenty-six or twenty-seven, is a growing, inchoate dissatisfaction, a yearning for more, even if her life is already quite full. Her apartment feels too quiet, her work, no matter how exciting or interesting, is less absorbing, and her spare time, unless packed with frenetic activities, almost echoes with loneliness—think of an endless wintry Sunday afternoon unbroken by the sound of another voice. She starts noticing the mothers all around her—especially young, attractive mothers—pushing strollers down the street, cooing at their babies in supermarkets, and loading up their shopping carts with enormous quantities of meat, vegetables, cans, jars, boxes of detergent, and packages of diapers, as she purchases a few meager items for her own dinner. All the horrors she once connected with babies—their noise and messiness, their garish plastic toys, their constant crying and demands that wear down and dull even the most strong-minded of women—are eclipsed by their previously underestimated virtues: their cuteness, their tiny shoes and mittens, their love and wonder, and, perhaps most enviable of all, the change of life they cause, pulling a woman out of herself and distracting her from her own familiar problems.

Alas, it is usually at precisely this moment—when a single woman looks up from her work and realizes she's ready to take on family life—that men make themselves most absent. This is when the cruelty of her singleness really sets in, when she becomes aware of the fine print in the unwritten bargain she has cut with the opposite sex. Men will outlast her. Men, particularly successful men, will be attractive and virile into their fifties. *They* can start families whenever they feel like it. So long as a woman was willing to play a man's game at dating—playing the field, holding men to no expectations of permanent commitment—men would be around; they would even live with her! But the moment she began exuding that desire for something more permanent, they'd vanish. I suspect that few things are more off-putting to a man eating dinner than to notice that the woman across the table is looking at him more hungrily than at the food on her plate—and she is not hungry for his body but for his whole life.

So the single woman is reduced to performing the romantic equivalent of a dance over hot coals: She must pretend that she is totally unaware of the burning rocks beneath her feet and behave in a way that will convince a man that the one thing she really wants is the furthest thing from her mind. She might feign indifference to his phone calls and insist she's busy when she's not. When visiting friends who have small children, she might smile at them or politely bat them away or ask questions about them as if they're a species of plant and she's not someone particularly interested in botany. Whatever she does, though, she cannot be blamed for believing, at this point in her life, that it is men who have benefited most from women's determination to remain independent. I often think that moderately attractive bachelors in their thirties now possess the sexual power that once belonged only to models and millionaires. They have their pick of companions, and may callously disregard the increasingly desperate thirtyish single women around them or move on when their current love becomes too cloying. As for the single woman over thirty, she may be in every other aspect of her life a paragon of female achievement; but in her romantic life, she must force herself to be as eager to please and accommodate male desire as any 1920s cotillion debutante.

This disparity in sexual staying power is something feminists rather recklessly overlooked when they urged women to abandon marriage and domesticity in favor of autonomy and self-fulfillment outside the home. The generation of women that embraced the feminist idealization of independence may have caused havoc by walking away from their marriages and families, but they could do so having established in their own mind that these were not the lives they wanted to lead: Those women at least *had* marriages and families from which to walk away. The thirty-three-year-old single woman who decides she wants more from life than her career cannot so readily walk *into* marriage and children; by postponing them, all she has done is to push them ahead to a point in her life when she has less sexual power to attain them. Instead, she must confront the sad possibility that she might never have what was the birthright of every previous generation of women: children, a home life, and a husband who—however dull or oppressive he might have appeared to feminist eyes—at least was *there.* As this older single woman's life stretches out before her, she'll wonder if she'll ever meet someone she could plausibly love and who will love her in return or whether she's condemned to making the rest of her journey on the train alone. She might have to forgo her hope of youthful marriage and the pleasure of starting out fresh in life with a husband at the same stage of the journey as herself. She may have to consider looking at men who are much older than she is, men on their second and third marriages who arrive with an assortment of heavy baggage and former traveling companions. These men may already have children and be uninterested in having more, or she'll have to patch together a new family out of broken ones. Or, as time passes and still no one comes along, this woman might join the other older single women in the waiting rooms of fertility clinics, the ones who hope science will now provide them with the babies that the pursuit of independence did not.

A WOMAN'S decision to delay marriage and children has other consequences—less obvious than the biological ones and therefore harder to foresee. It is not simply the pressure of wanting a baby that turns those confident twenty-five-year-old single career women you see striding through busy intersections at lunch hour, wearing sleek suits and carrying take-out salads to eat at their desks, into the morose, white-wine-drinking thirty-five-year-old executives huddled around restaurant tables, frantically analyzing every quality about themselves that might be contributing to their stubbornly unsuccessful romantic lives. By spending years and years living entirely for yourself, thinking only about yourself, and having responsibility to no one but yourself, you end up inadvertently extending the introverted existence of a teenager deep into middle age. The woman who avoids permanent commitment because she fears it will stunt her development as an individual may be surprised to realize in her thirties that having essentially the same life as she did at eighteen—the same dating problems, the same solitary habits, the same anxieties about her future, and the same sense that her life has not yet fully begun—is stunting, too.

When a woman postpones marriage and motherhood, she does not end up thinking about love less as she gets older but more and more, sometimes to the point of obsession. Why am I still alone? she wonders. Why can't I find someone? What is *wrong* with me? Her friends who have married are getting on with their lives—they are putting down payments on cars and homes; babies are arriving. She may not like some of their marriages—she may think her best friend's husband is a bit of a jerk or that another one of her friends has changed for the worse since her marriage—but nonetheless, she will think that at least their lives are going forward while her gearshift remains stuck in neutral. The more time that passes, the more the gearshift rattles, the more preoccupied the woman becomes with herself and all her possible shortcomings in the eyes of men until she can think about little else.

This may be the joke that history has actually played upon us—and a nasty one it is. Switch on the television or wander into a bookstore and it is striking how many programs and books are now aimed at a market of thirtyish single women who are unhappy and fretful about their solitary state. What is fascinating about the self-help books in particular is not so much the advice they give but the reader their authors believe they are speaking to—a reader who scarcely existed a generation ago. This woman is not using her hard-won freedom and her hard-won money to move beyond herself and her immediate personal problems. She is using it, rather, to delve ever more deeply into herself, buying up volume after volume of cheap psychology that only pushes her further into nail-biting introspection. While the authors of these books attempt to differentiate their theories by offering pseudoscientific systems (measuring their readers' "pleasure pattern" or "receptivity to love") or dividing single women into tidy psychological categories ("the Sexual Martyr," "the Co-Dependent," etc.), the conclusion that emerges is always the same: Millions of women need constant reassurance about their self-worth.

The authors of the 1996 best-selling how-to-catch-a-husband book, *The Rules*, took for granted a readership of single women so neurotically self-absorbed, so desperately out of control, that they needed to be reminded of such things as not to "babble on and on" to their dates, not to reveal "that getting married is foremost on your mind," and not to stay on the phone with men "for an hour or two recounting your feelings or every incident of the day." As feminist writer Katha Pollitt cruelly put it in a review of the book: "The woman depicted as in need of *The Rules* is a voracious doormat, the sort of woman who sends men Hallmark greeting cards or long letters after a single date, who rummages in men's drawers and pockets, suggests couples therapy when brief relationships start to crumble, throws away a new boyfriend's old clothes, cleans (and redecorates) his apartment without asking, and refuses to see the most obvious signs of disengagement." Pollitt gamely goes on to argue that the woman who behaves like this does so only because she is not a confident feminist who has learned to value her own company. "Her problem isn't too much liberation; it's incredibly low self-esteem," she writes. And that incredibly low self-esteem has to be a product, of course, of this sexist world we live in, one in which men and women continue to "need" each other only for such superficial reasons as "acceptability in a society organized around the couple." It would not occur to someone like Pollitt that a woman might be driven to this kind of behavior precisely *because* she has spent her adulthood relentlessly pursuing the feminist goal of independence and now feels so inescapably independent that it's driving her nuts.

Yet the self-help gurus, even those who aren't avowedly feminist, by and large agree with Pollitt. In book after book, they repeat the stereotypical feminist attitude of the past thirty years—that any form of dependence upon a man is potentially harmful and unhealthy to a woman's identity. "Many women still end up in relationships where their wants, beliefs, priorities, and ambitions are compromised under relationship pressures," writes the best-selling author Harriet Lerner in *Life Preservers*. "The best way to work on an intimate relationship is to work on the *self*." "If you spend more time worrying what others think than working on what you want or need, you will always be disappointed," warns Dr. Wayne Dyer in his book *Erroneous Zones*, which has sold more than 6 million copies. Its cover exclaims: "Dyer shows that only *you* can make yourself happy and points the way to true self-reliance [italics mine]."

This level of self-absorption, however, has the perverse effect of making it even more difficult ever to attract, let alone keep, someone. (As the single heroine of Helen Fielding's 1996 novel, *Bridget Jones' Diary*, resolves to herself: "I will not sulk about having no boyfriend, but develop inner poise and authority and sense of self as woman of substance, complete *without* boyfriend, as best way to obtain boyfriend.") My single male friends in their thirties complain about going on dates with women who spend the entire evening talking about themselves and analyzing themselves aloud. These women are no longer capable, it seems, of holding a general conversation or of even *feigning interest* in a general conversation. They've become female versions of the eccentric bachelor—like Professor Higgins or his modern-day equivalent, Jerry Seinfeld—who are so set in their quirky habits, perverse likes and dislikes, and long-standing relationships with equally eccentric friends, that they cannot seriously involve themselves with anyone else. Instead—like the chronically single TV character Ally McBeal, who exclaims, "I like being a mess. It's who I am"—their problems now define their personalities; and without these problems, they wouldn't know who they are. A horrified *Time* magazine put Ally McBeal on its June 1998 cover over the headline "Is Feminism Dead?" To the editors of *Time*, the character of McBeal, in her self-absorption and sex-craziness, betrayed everything the women's movement was supposed to stand for. But what after all could better express the spirit of feminist autonomy than this line from another of *Time*'s traitors to her sex, the confessional author Elizabeth Wurtzel, in her 1998 book, *Bitch: In Praise of Difficult Women*: "I intend to scream, shout, throw tantrums in Bloomingdale's if I feel like it and confess intimate details of my life to complete strangers. I intend to answer only to myself."

FROM A FEMINIST view, it would be nice, I suppose—or at the very least handy—if we were able to derive total satisfaction from our solitude, to be entirely self-contained organisms, like earthworms or amoebas, having relations with the opposite sex whenever we felt a need for it but otherwise being entirely contented with our own company. Every woman's apartment could be her Walden Pond. She'd be free of the romantic fuss and interaction that has defined, and given meaning to, human existence since its creation. She could spend her evenings happily ensconced with a book or a rented video, not having to deal with some bozo's desire to watch football or play mindless video games. How children would fit into this vision of autonomy, I'm not sure, but surely they would infringe upon it; perhaps she could simply farm them out. If this seems a rather chilling outcome to the quest for independence, well, it is. If no man is an island, then no woman can be, either. And it's why most human beings fall in love, and continue to take on all the commitments and responsibilities of family life. We *want* the warm body next to us on the sofa in the evenings; we *want* the noise and embrace of family around us; we *want*, at the end of our lives, to look back and see that what we have done amounts to more than a pile of pay stubs, that we have loved and been loved, and brought into this world life that will outlast us.

The quest for autonomy—the need "to be oneself" or, as Wurtzel declares, the intention "to answer only to myself"—is in fact not a brave or noble one; nor is it an indication of strong character. Too often, autonomy is merely the excuse of someone who is so fearful, so weak, that he or she can't bear to take on any of the responsibilities that used to be shouldered by much younger but more robust and mature souls. I'm struck by the number of my single contemporaries—men and women in their early to mid-thirties—who speak of themselves as if they were still twenty years old, just embarking upon their lives and not, as they actually are, already halfway through them. In another era, a thirty-three-year-old man or woman might have already lived through a depression and a world war and had several children. Yet at the suggestion of marriage—or of buying a house or of having a baby—these modern thirtysomethings will exclaim, "But I'm so young!" their crinkled eyes widening at the thought. In the relationships they do have—even "serious" ones—they will take pains to avoid the appearance of anything that smacks of permanent commitment. The strange result is couples who are willing to share *everything* with each other—leases, furniture, cars, weekends, body fluids, holidays with their relatives—just as long as it comes with the right to cancel the relationship *at any moment.*

Unfortunately, postponing marriage and all the responsibilities that go with it does not prolong youth. It only prolongs the illusion of it, and then again only in one's own eyes. The traits that are forgivable in a twenty-year-old—the constant wondering about who you are and what you will be; the readiness to chuck one thing, or person, for another and move on—are less attractive in a thirty-two-year-old. More often what results is a middle-aged person who retains all the irritating self-absorption of an adolescent without gaining any of the redeeming qualities of maturity. Those qualities—wisdom, a sense of duty, the willingness to make sacrifices for others, an acceptance of aging and death—are qualities that spring directly from our relationships and commitments to others.

A woman will not understand what true dependency is until she is cradling her own infant in her arms; nor will she likely achieve the self-confidence she craves until she has withstood, and transcended, the weight of responsibility a family places upon her—a weight that makes all the paperwork and assignments of her in-basket seem feather-light. The same goes for men. We strengthen a muscle by using it, and that is true of the heart and mind, too. By waiting and waiting and waiting to commit to someone, our capacity for love shrinks and withers. This doesn't mean that women or men should marry the first reasonable person to come along, or someone with whom they are not in love. But we should, at a much earlier age than we do now, take a serious attitude toward dating and begin preparing ourselves to settle down. For it's in the act of taking up the roles we've been taught to avoid or postpone—wife, husband, mother, father—that we build our identities, expand our lives, and achieve the fullness of character we desire.

Still, critics may argue that the old way was no better; that the risk of loss women assume by delaying marriage and motherhood overbalances the certain loss we'd suffer by marrying too early. The habit of viewing marriage as a raw deal for women is now so entrenched, even among women who don't call themselves feminists, that I've seen brides who otherwise appear completely happy apologize to their wedding guests for their surrender to convention, as if a part of them still feels there is something embarrassing and weak about an intelligent and ambitious woman consenting to marry. But is this true? Or is it just an alibi we've been handed by the previous generation of women in order to justify the sad, lonely outcomes of so many lives?

What we rarely hear—or perhaps are too fearful to admit—is how *liberating* marriage can actually be. As nerve-racking as making the decision can be, it is also an enormous relief once it is made. The moment we say, "I do," we have answered one of the great, crucial questions of our lives: We now know with whom we'll be spending the rest of our years, who will be the father of our children, who will be our family. That our marriages may not work, that we will have to accommodate ourselves to the habits and personality of someone else—these are, and always have been, the risks of commitment, of love itself. What is important is that our lives have been thrust forward. The negative—that we are no longer able to live entirely for ourselves—is also the positive: *We no longer have to live entirely for ourselves!* We may go on to do any number of interesting things, but we are free of the gnawing wonder of *with whom* we will do them. We have ceased to look down the tunnel, waiting for a train.

The pull between the desire to love and be loved and the desire to be free is an old, fierce one. If the error our grandmothers made was to have surrendered too much of themselves for others, this was perhaps better than not being prepared to surrender anything at all. The fear of losing oneself can, in the end, simply become an excuse for not giving any of oneself away. Generations of women may have had no choice but to commit themselves to marriage early and then to feel imprisoned by their lifelong domesticity. So many of our generation have decided to put it off until it is too late, not foreseeing that lifelong independence can be its own kind of prison, too.

chapter three

About Marriage

MARRIED WOMEN in the 1970s often became feminists after having what they described as a "click" experience. Their husbands handed them one too many dirty shirts to launder. They were ignored at yet another party because as "wives of" they were assumed to have nothing to say. Or one day, as they drove their kids from soccer practice to piano class, it hit them that they had not earned degrees in history or English only to become the unpaid chauffeurs of whiny eight-year-olds. What am I doing with my life? they'd wonder. And then it would all "click." They'd been passively accepting a role forced upon them by a society run for the benefit of their husbands. From now on, it was going to be different: They were going to start putting their own desires and dreams ahead of their families'. Whether these women eventually got a divorce or took jobs didn't matter. The point was that they understood, in the flash of a second, why their lives seemed so terribly wrong and unfulfilling. The personal *is* the political!

Not long ago, I had what might be called the opposite of a "click" experience (a "clack" experience?). My husband and I were attending a weekly tennis clinic held at a college campus down the street from where we live. During one session, as the instructor assembled a group of us by the net, I realized that I'd left my tennis racket on a bench at the other end of the

court. I noticed my husband had left his, too. I jogged quickly to the
bench and retrieved both rackets.

"Oh darn," remarked one of our classmates as I rejoined the group.
She was a woman who looked to be in her early thirties. "I was going to
congratulate you for *not* bringing it."

"Sorry?" I didn't follow her meaning.

"Your husband's racket," she explained. "I was hoping you were going
to make him get it himself."

"Ah." Now I "clacked." Her tone was jovial enough and, so far as I
could tell, she meant no hostility toward my husband, whom she'd only
just met. But her offhand joke was a perfect example of how fully the notion "the personal is the political" has come to be accepted in even the
most trivial exchanges between men and women, and in particular between husbands and wives. In my classmate's eyes, bringing my husband
his racket was thoughtful, sure, but also an action that might betray some
lingering, reactionary belief on my part that it is the wife's *duty* to bring
her husband his things. What sort of behavior would I be capable of next?
Fetching him his newspaper and slippers? Having a chilled martini ready
for him when he came home from work? Safer not to bring him anything
at all—*let him get his own damn racket!*

But imagine the situation the other way around. How would I have reacted if my husband had returned with his racket but left mine on the
bench? And what if he'd made it clear that he did so because he didn't
want me to get the idea that it was his job to bring me things? I would
think he was a boor—and not just a boor, but the very kind of sexist boor
we are told most men were before they were enlightened by the women's
movement. Hadn't generations of husbands relied upon the crudest assumptions about female nature—"You can never trust them"/"They'll
walk all over you if you let them"—to bully their wives and keep them in
their place? Now here was my otherwise perfectly pleasant classmate reflexively espousing the same sort of boorish sexism in reverse: You can
never trust a man. He'll walk all over you if you let him. You've got to
keep him in his place.

Yet what surprised me most about my classmate's remark was not so much its attitude but that it came from someone my own age. We are not, after all, the generation of women who had to join "consciousness-raising" groups or go "on strike" in our homes in order to get men to take us more seriously. The sort of husband who demands supper on the table, who tells the little woman to shut up until she's spoken to, who declares, while settling into his armchair and popping open a beer, that a woman's place is in the home—who, in short, would *not* get the damn racket himself—is by now as much an outdated caricature as those housewives chirping over the miracle of their new dryers in old advertisements from *The Saturday Evening Post*. This isn't to say that a certain kind of old-fashioned, sexist male is entirely extinct. But to the degree that he exists, he is a dinosaur—one who may still rove through a few conservative pockets of the country, or hide in orthodox religious enclaves, or lurk behind the odd office desk, on the verge of retirement. Men today—particularly all those dads you see out on Sunday mornings with babies strapped to their chests, buying their wearied working wives take-out cappuccinos—would not even dare to hope that their wives would have supper on the table, let alone bring *them* a coffee while they slept in.

Yet the habit of viewing all husbands as potential oppressors is deeply ingrained. That men may be doing an unprecedented share of the housework and child rearing, that they may respect their wives' ambitions and individuality, is not nearly enough to allay women's anxieties that they risk losing their identities and might turn into domestic drudges as soon as they marry. When *McCall's* asked its readers in a 1992 survey, "Do you feel you gave up a part of your true self [when you married]?" hundreds wrote in to say yes. Respondents to a similar poll by *New Woman* magazine said they believed, by a margin of 83 percent, that "wives submerge a vital part of themselves."

These anxieties, however, do not match the facts. The Gallup company has done periodic surveys over the past fifty years of male and female attitudes toward housework. It found that 85 percent of married people today say the husband helps with the housework, 73 percent say he helps with cooking, and 57 percent say he helps with the dishes. (Interestingly enough, in the Bad Old Days of 1949, the poll found that 62 percent of husbands helped with the housework, 40 percent with the cooking, and 31 percent with the dishes.) Men's increased involvement in the house further reflects quite a staggering change in their attitudes toward domestic roles in general. Every year since 1973, the University of Michigan's Institute for Social Research has conducted extensive surveys on high school seniors. In recent surveys, the vast majority (76 percent) of these young men agreed with the idea that "having a job gives a wife more of a chance to develop herself as a person"; that women should have the same education and job opportunities as men (73 percent); and that parents should encourage independence in their daughters just as much as they do in their sons (78 percent). They also agreed that if a wife works, her husband should take a greater part in the housework and child care (72 percent) and that in general, "most fathers should spend more time with their children than they do now" (78 percent).

And yet despite this remarkable evolution, *women* persist in viewing *men* in old-fashioned, stereotypical ways. As Gallup also reported, "Perceptions about which half of the marriage partnership dominates the other have shifted dramatically *against* men: today, husbands are seen as more likely to dominate their wives [39 percent of women felt this way vs. 26 percent], while shortly after [World War II] most Americans saw little difference or, when they did, they perceived *wives* as more likely to dominate their husbands [italics mine]." The male researcher who released Gallup's findings went on to add, a wee bit sarcastically, "It may seem to many men that when it comes to gender roles in the household, they can't win for losing."

A woman might reply to this little aside with, So what? Men are helping around the house more, but they are still not doing as much as women. And this would be fair comment if the argument were simply about equal divisions of labor in the household. But it isn't. The Gallup employee makes a fair point. American women have achieved the most egalitarian marriages in the history of the world. And yet they actually feel *more* oppressed in their marriages than their grandmothers did. How is this possible?

In some ways, I suppose, it's not that startling. The fierce independence a woman pursues throughout her youth is not going to be easily surrendered at the altar—no matter how happy a woman may be about getting married, no matter how much in love with her husband. If she does seek to do more in life than be a wife and mother, somewhere within herself she will view her decision to marry as a surrender. The queasiness she may feel about walking down the aisle in full bridal regalia, her nervousness about the role of wife, is in part the residual effect of nearly two centuries of protests by women against marriage. Ever since Mary Wollstonecraft dipped her pen in ink to write *The Vindication of the Rights of Woman* in 1792, we have heard over and over again that marriage is an institution created for the benefit of men at the expense of women's freedom. The contemporary feminists who condemn the *Ozzie and Harriet* household are simply repeating the latest version of a viewpoint that has not changed much since Victorian suffragettes raged in their overstuffed drawing rooms against women's enslavement by their husbands. They echo Simone de Beauvoir, who wrote in her 1949 treatise, *The Second Sex*, that marriage is "intended to deny [a woman] a man's liberty" and that a wife's function is nothing more than "to satisfy a male's sexual needs and to take care of his household" in exchange for his protection. That marriage may, in our time, no longer bear much resemblance to de Beauvoir's grim version of it is fully beside the point. This idea of marriage is as familiar to us as our husbands' faults.

Women are understandably eager to hear the men-are-to-blame argument. Who can deny that women, despite all the progress they have made outside the home, continue to be more burdened than men by the things that go on within it? It's women who still take charge of the children and their schedules. It's women who will take a cut in hours and pay to gain more time away from the office. It's women who are still impinged upon by the daily domestic worries—keeping track of the plumber's appointment, noticing that the kitchen is low on paper towels and that nothing has been defrosted for dinner *again*. To a generation raised to believe in the absolute equality of the sexes, the sacrifices and accommodations that women continue to make in marriage seem arbitrary and unfair. In marriages in which both husband and wife work, why *should* women still do more of the household chores? Why *do* we assume that it will be the mother, and not the father, who will crimp her work and her ambitions for the sake of the children?

And the unfairness, a married woman soon discovers, goes much more deeply than this. It does not just extend to what her husband or the society around her expects her to do but, more subtly, to her *own* impulse to do things and make sacrifices for her husband and family. Gloria Steinem called this impulse women's "compassion disease"—the need to take care of everyone around you, fetch soup for the sick, and put others' problems ahead of your own. It's the same impulse that Virginia Woolf ridiculed in the Victorian wife—the kind who made so many sacrifices in such "charming" and "unselfish" ways that "in short she was so constituted that she never had a mind or wish of her own, but preferred to sympathize always with the minds and wishes of others." Whatever we may call it, the impulse has survived the past quarter century of women "clicking" and telling men to do things themselves. And it startles no one more than the woman who has spent her single years avoiding compromise and commitment; who has managed to maintain in her romantic life the same strictly equal relationships with men that she enjoys in her professional life. Suddenly, all the domestic urges she feels upon marriage—her desire to make a home, to have children—collide with her nervousness about losing her independence. These urges clash, too, with her perception of herself as a modern woman. The realization that she has the capacity *within herself* to surrender to the role of Wife is genuinely frightening—so frightening, in fact, that it may inhibit her from getting married at all.

I've known several accomplished women, all contemporaries of mine, who lived with their boyfriends for several years before marrying them—not because they didn't love these men or were uncertain about them and not because the men themselves weren't willing to get married, but because the women fretted over what marriage itself might do to their personalities. It was as if they imagined they'd be cast under a spell the moment they accepted a ring and turned into some hellish vision they had of the domesticated woman—a woman who gets her exercise from vacuuming and dusting, who coos incessantly over her husband and all his little virtues, who is the joyful recipient of electric pepper mills and food processors at Christmas. So long as these women avoided marriage, they believed, they could enjoy all of the benefits of companionship and romantic intimacy without sacrificing the rigid egalitarianism they'd established as a childless, unmarried couple. Like college roommates, they split the bills with their boyfriends, scrupulously divided the household chores, held different bank accounts, kept up demanding hours at their jobs, and sometimes took separate vacations. At the same time, though, these women expected to be treated socially as married couples—to be invited together to events with their boyfriends and to have their lovers welcomed at holiday celebrations as "one of the family" even if, from the family's point of view, this person could be gone by next Thursday.

When, after years of living like this, the pressure increased upon these women to marry (and, ironically, in their case it was not simply biological pressure but came from their boyfriends—men who were reaching the peak of their careers and, with their hairlines beginning to gray or recede, were restless to start families), they'd give in, but only with great amounts of eye-rolling and ironic jokes about the dull-witted wives they surely risked turning into. I remember one couple who announced their engagement at a dinner party: The man looked positively elated, bursting with romantic pride, while his girlfriend smiled weakly, disparaged all offers of congratulation, and spent the remainder of the evening staring grimly into her wineglass like a condemned woman.

IN ATTEMPTING to redress marriage's perceived unfairness to women, our society has taken steps, many of them quite reasonable, to make marriage more equally balanced. It seems astonishing now that a woman of my mother's generation could not borrow money or apply for a credit card without her husband's permission, or that in the event of a divorce, a court—not to mention her female friends—would treat her adultery more seriously than her husband's. My mother's stories of the stigma suffered by married middle-class women who worked—that it was thought somehow improper, that it deprived a family man who needed the job more—may as well be stories of how women once lacked the right to vote, so far away do those attitudes seem now. More impressive than any legal reform are the changes in the day-to-day division of labor between husbands and wives: changes that have come about partly out of expediency, with husbands doing more around the house to compensate for the fact that their wives now spend a larger portion of their time at offices; but changes, too, that are the result of men's genuine respect and support for women's aspirations. Very few men today would have the nerve to present their new brides with a large basket of socks that needed darning, as Calvin Coolidge did shortly after he and his wife returned from their honeymoon. Nor would any woman cheerfully accept it, as did Mrs. Coolidge. I think it's safe to say that there has been no generation of men raised with fewer expectations of what their wives will do for them than the current one. They don't expect—or should I say take for granted—that their wives will cook for them, clean their houses, care for their children, sew their buttons, or press their shirts. They don't presume that their wives will perform *any* domestic chores simply because they are women. The prenegotiated deal of our grandparents that de Beauvoir lambasted—he works, she runs the house—is no longer the standard.

Instead, when a couple marries they must negotiate their own set of rules—their own domestic treaty, as it were. In many cases—particularly when a couple does not have children—these individually worked out arrangements have produced terms that would pass the muster of the Fair Labor Standards Act. Tasks are divided equally, according to convenience and a person's inclination and only incidentally according to sex. If the husband loaded the dishwasher at breakfast, the wife will do it at dinner, and vice versa. Some nights, he cooks and she washes up. On other nights, she cooks and he washes up. He does the grocery shopping because he has time that week; on other weeks, when she has time, she does the grocery shopping. When children come along, it becomes trickier to maintain the appearance of equality because there are so many more tasks that only the wife can do (like breast-feeding) or because she's the one at home on maternity leave. But modern couples have found ways to adjust for this, too. If she minds the baby during the day, he might take over at night. Or maybe she feeds the baby lunch and afternoon bottles, he gives the breakfast and dinnertime bottles, and whoever is the least tired gives the nighttime bottle. If she changed the diaper last time, now it's his turn. I've noticed that even in marriages superficially more traditional in form, in which a woman stays home with the kids and her husband works, a woman may do more of the day-to-day chores than her husband but will still expect him to make up for his absence when he comes home and do *all* the evening chores. I know of no husband who is permitted—as his grandfather would have been—to put his feet up or his nose in the newspaper or fall asleep in front of the television while his wife gets dinner and distracts the baby.

After my first child was born, my mother frequently made two envious observations: the superiority of modern baby equipment and the superiority of modern fathers. In her day, she reminded me, the garden-variety middle-class father would *not* come home early from the office when the kids were sick, would *not* change a diaper, would *not* watch the kids on Saturday afternoon—or if he did, he would bestow a two-hour break with the magnanimity of a ducal favor. The modern dad—the one giving a bottle in an airport lounge, or reading a grocery list in a supermarket aisle with a baby reaching from the cart, or enthusiastically toting the children off to the playground—was, in my mother's eyes, as remarkable an improvement as the ultrathin disposable diapers and battery-operated baby swings. One weekend, when I took my son to another three-year-old's birthday party, I was amused to notice that virtually every one of the dads in attendance was walking around jiggling a baby on his hip or shoulders while the wives, all businesswomen, collected together in the living room to drink wine and discuss their jobs.

So marriage has been transformed. That it may not be transformed *enough* is another problem. A woman who is accustomed to viewing herself as an entirely liberated creature will be entirely unprepared to take full charge of traditional chores like cooking or the laundry, no matter how helpful and diligent her husband may be. And, of course, few husbands will ever be *perfectly* helpful and diligent. So when these chores do fall—despite extraordinary pressure to the contrary—along traditional sexual lines, that is an added source of tension to the marriage—unless the woman can persuade herself that she does the vacuuming, say, or most of the child care because she *wants* to or because she's *better at it* and not because her husband thinks that it's *her job*. Any suggestion otherwise, no matter how unintentional, might cause her to snap. The husband who incautiously asks his wife to iron his shirt or wash his gym clothes may find himself suddenly being rebuked: Does he, at some subconscious Neanderthal level of his brain, really think that she is more biologically suited to pressing collars and laundering his smelly shorts? What does he think she does at the law firm all day? Debate over brands of detergent? Or the woman who cooked her lover romantic dinners while they were dating may suddenly balk at cooking him dinner after they are married, lest her husband develop any expectation that she *ought* to cook him dinner. He might unwisely express genuine surprise: What happened to all those great meals I used to get? And she will resent the sexism of his presumption.

As a result of this lingering suspicion of men, and of ourselves, a great many married women find themselves unable—or unwilling—to make even very commonplace accommodations to married life. This resistance persists regardless of how accomplished, how beautiful, or how important these women are in their own right, and they are intensified if she is married to a powerful man. Anyone who followed the tragic saga of the late Princess of Wales was constantly made to understand, by those sympathetic to the Princess, how Diana's royal duties and obligations as wife of the heir to the British throne stifled her identity as an individual. Patricia Duff, the gorgeous wife of billionaire Ron Perelman, refused to take her new husband's name, and kept a separate office and vacation house from him, before finally divorcing him. Donna Hanover Giuliani, wife of New York City mayor Rudy Giuliani, began turning down political and charitable events halfway through his first term because, as her press secretary told *The New York Times,* "she [Mrs. Giuliani] wants to be acknowledged for being her own person, and not for being somebody's partner." Obviously, there is great marital unhappiness woven into these stories, but this is not how the women involved chose to portray it—not to others, and perhaps not even to themselves. Such women don't say, "My husband and I have real differences that we are trying to work out," but offer, more vaguely, "I'm finding it hard to be myself." It is a convenient, modern excuse for marital unhappiness, one that removes blame and responsibility from the woman and casts it upon the husband, who is, by nature of his sex, presumed to have the more forceful, dominant, and thus oppressive personality. The woman is viewed as victim, no matter how much her own behavior might be to blame for the trouble in her marriage.

The Diana-Duff-Giuliani phenomenon was described well, for more ordinary mortals, in a 1997 book called *The Marriage Shock: The Transformation of Women into Wives,* by Dalma Heyn, a former executive editor of *McCall's.* Heyn interviewed dozens of newly married young women about their reactions to their wedded state. Marriage, Heyn concluded, "could not be less natural for many women today. The average young woman—working, assertive, personally and professionally—is comfortable with independence, employment, autonomy, and multiple sexual relationships. She is as used to pleasure as to pleasing, and envisions having both in equal measure in an egalitarian marital relationship."

The unhappy "shock" for an unsuspecting modern woman like this, according to Heyn, occurs within the first few months of marriage. The women with whom she spoke found themselves being overtaken by what might be called "getting the tennis racket" syndrome, and began a kind of Dr. Jekyll mutation into the wives they thought they'd never become. "When Judy noticed something was different when she married, she asked her married friends, 'Is the first year always like this?' " wrote Heyn. "She heard an astonishing number of embarrassed yeses. [Yet] rather than face the terrifying questions 'What's the matter with me?' and 'What do I do now?' [Judy] decides 'it' will pass; 'it' is nothing. 'It' is what they mean by 'compromise' and she'll get used to it. . . . She will, as they all promise, 'adjust.' " But in the adjusting, Judy becomes, as the author puts it, "deeply, profoundly, not like herself."

Heyn went on to relate with great sympathy the sacrifices these women felt they had made by getting married. What was startling about these interviews, however, was not the enormity of the compromises the women described but the relentless pettiness of them. Few of the women Heyn spoke to, for instance, had yet to face motherhood. They had not given up their careers. They were comfortably well-off. They had all married men who, on the whole, sounded like models of enlightenment and were anxious for their wives' well-being. What seemed to bother the women most, as they spelled it out, were the compromises inherent in the act of marriage itself—that they should be expected to adjust their behavior to suit another person in *any way*.

So a forty-year-old woman named Elaine remembered her honeymoon like a political dissident recalling the imposition of martial law. Elaine, Heyn writes, "tried hard to locate that moment when she first altered her normal behavior even slightly, when she covered over a word or a thought somewhat, adjusted an observation, an opinion, a feeling, or a demand, spoke in a more moderated voice or made a more giving, compliant, or censorious move: 'It was the night after we got married.' " Another wife, Tracy, sadly told the story of attending her husband's office Christmas party shortly after they were married. Suddenly she realized it might be inappropriate for her to dress in a leather miniskirt and jump around the dance floor with her husband's unmarried colleagues. Instead, she thought, she ought to wear something more "proper" and spend time getting to know her husband's boss. She did it, but only resentfully, "wistfully" listening to the music in the background and glumly watching the secretaries, thinking "how sexy and lively they looked, so different from the wives!" A woman named Antonia expressed her unhappiness that she could no longer share with her husband all the frank details of her sexual past, even though she had done so while they were dating. "He was more uptight about my old boyfriends, and even my former husband, after we married," she confided. This stifling of her "sexual openness" caused her to become more circumspect and imposed upon her "a strange new shame," one that led her into "shyness and repression." A woman called Karen described feeling "dissent in the pit of her stomach" when she was introduced by her married name instead of her maiden one. Although she decided not to challenge it—by "rationalizing," Heyn wrote, that it's "just a tired old feminist issue"—she still felt her "stomach . . . tightening every time she [was] called by [her husband's] name and [didn't] speak up about it." Adrienne, a New York art historian, told Heyn that the minute after she married she thought " 'What do I do now? I know, I'll cook!' I had learned what was expected of me. I don't think it was [my husband] who told me, I just knew. I didn't want to go along with it, but I did, because I knew that I couldn't be a wife and still be really, really me."

As Adrienne and the other women acknowledged, none of these feelings of oppression were provoked by sexist or even thoughtless behavior of their husbands. Indeed Tracy's husband, we are told, was dismayed by his wife's new restraint: He was sorry she gave away her leather miniskirt and he spent the evening at the Christmas party urging her to dance with his friends. Another woman, who said she "renounced something" of herself in marriage but didn't "know quite what it is," candidly admitted that if she were to tell her husband, "Honey, I feel I'm giving up too much for our marriage," he'd be "flabbergasted." Yet Heyn expends no pages in her book discussing the compromises that husbands make for their wives. She has nothing to say about the "shock" men might suffer from marriage to women whose behavior radically and mysteriously changes the moment they slip on a ring. Heyn doesn't seriously consider the man's point of view at all.

And in this way her book amounts to a nearly perfect cultural snapshot of late-twentieth-century middle-class marriage. So preoccupied are women with what *they* lose in marriage, so certain of the fact that they *do* lose in marriage, that they no longer even bother to ask themselves what their husbands give up, if anything. Reading Heyn's book, I found myself trying to imagine whether a male equivalent of it could be published and, if so, what women would think of it. Could we be as sympathetic if it were men who were revealing their fear of "losing" their identities in marriage? Would we be willing to encourage husbands in their "right" to be themselves—to spend their money as they liked, to stay out all night playing poker and drinking beer with the guys, to flirt with other women, to watch television when they got home instead of speaking to us, to stop taking out the garbage and mowing the lawn, and to quit a boring and un-fulfilling job when the rent is due and the new baby is crying? And what about all the little lies that husbands are forced to tell—lies that might "compromise" their own feelings of sexual honesty? "Really, blondes with big breasts just aren't my type"; "Seriously, I never think about her anymore"; "Honey, you look *terrific* in that bathing suit!" Perhaps Heyn doesn't think about any of this because, simply, she can't think about it. The immense changes in men and their marital expectations are so threatening to her theories that they must be ignored. And in this Heyn is typical of contemporary feminists. Even a Pulitzer Prize–winning jour-nalist like Susan Faludi somehow does not see the Snugli-wearing dads and dishwashing husbands around her. Instead, she laments that "while a revolution has gone on in the hearts and minds of women, no such revo-lution has taken place in the hearts and minds of men."

Gloria Steinem once joked that we have become "the husbands we wanted to marry," but maybe the truth is that we are in danger of becom-ing the husbands we left behind: balky, self-absorbed, and supremely sure that our needs should come before anyone else's. And no matter how en-titled some women feel to such behavior, it will hardly help us to achieve the lasting, happy marriages most of us still profess to want. Modern women often complain that they are baffled by their own lives: At pre-cisely the moment they feel that they've purged themselves of all their self-doubt and personal weakness—when they at last feel themselves ready for a serious relationship with a man—no men, or should I say no *marriageable* men, seem anywhere in sight. Or when we do get married, we congratulate ourselves that our marriages are much more fair and equal than those of our parents and then wonder why our marriages don't last. Puzzled by this mystery, we read articles and listen to experts, who advise us to demand ever more fairness, ever more equality, ever more autonomy in our relationships. In fact, of course, the only mystery here is how we have managed to make ourselves so blind. If good marriages seem more unattainable than ever before, it is because of our determination to remain as separate and distinct individuals within an institution that demands the opposite from us, that insists upon the merging of identity—of both husband and wife—if it is to be sustained.

Thus we now have the custom, among educated career women, of keeping their maiden name after they get married; indeed, they keep it as reflexively as their own grandmothers would have changed theirs to their husbands'. I've sat through many weddings that are traditional in all respects but this one. In everyday life, the bride may be a cutthroat attorney or network television producer, but on her wedding day she's prepared to embrace most of the old-fashioned symbolism: She may have had twenty previous lovers but she will pledge herself to her husband wearing virginal white tulle; she may have left home long ago and from Monday to Friday pull in a salary that makes her own father gasp, but on this day she will allow him the appearance of giving her away; and though she might have signed a prenuptial agreement covering every contingency of marital dissolution, she will vow to stay with her lover, for better or worse, until death. Yet when it comes to taking her husband's name—the traditional symbol of leaving behind one's past identity in order to assume a new joint one—she can't stomach it. It's one thing to put on a white gown for a day and repeat dusty vows, quite another to permanently dispense with the most prominent symbol of her autonomy. For this sort of woman to *give up* her maiden name amounts almost to an act of civil disobedience. I remember when a friend of mine, a very accomplished businesswoman, decided to take her husband's name: A few weeks after the wedding, she went into an upscale stationery store in New York to order new letterhead under her married name. The saleswoman became very huffy about my friend's decision. "None of *my* girls," she insisted, referring to her other female clients, "take their husbands' names."

It may seem trivial, but in its way the name issue reflects most deeply our loss of understanding of what marriage is about. And it also underscores, with every new introduction, the schizophrenia of the modern woman's identity. "Hello, I'm—" *Who?* If a woman keeps her maiden name, she will in fact set herself apart from being Mrs. His Wife, but she will also set herself apart from her own children, who may be puzzled why she doesn't have the same name as them. Go through the student directory of any private school and you will see the problem: Under the listings of parents, a few of the mothers who use their maiden names will hyphenate their children's names with their own, but mostly the father and the children are identified by one name, with the mother identified as Ms. Someone Else. As a result, the woman doesn't simply appear distinct "in her own right"; she appears separate from her own family, as if she's drawn a line in the sand between herself and them, one that she must draw over and over with every new introduction: "This is Mr. Serbia, Junior Serbia, Sally Serbia, and oh yes, over here is Ms. Bosnia-Herzegovina. She'd like the UN to formally recognize her independence." It's also a decision that causes a constant inner split among the women who make it. In my own marriage, for instance, I legally and socially took my husband's name, but continued to write under my maiden name. We're both journalists and frequently contribute to the same magazines, and using my maiden name as a byline seemed a good way to distinguish my own work from his while allowing me, in every other aspect of my life, to embrace my new familial name. But over time, this distinction has proven illusory, and has promoted an odd chasm between my identity as a writer and my identity as an individual. On paper I am one person; to everyone who matters to me most, I am someone else. When I meet people at parties or conferences, or any place for that matter, my mind is thrown into a sudden state of confusion as it juggles who I am at that moment: If it's social, I give my married name; if it's business, I use my maiden name, or string both awkwardly together. But given the politics that now attaches itself to keeping or changing one's name, in some ways I wish I'd made the decision when I married to change it entirely.

For keeping one's name is a kind of gauntlet that a woman throws down at the outset of her marriage, letting the world—and her husband—know that she plans to challenge the arrangement of the traditional marriage. The irony, though, is that this same woman may actually want traditional benefits from her marriage, whether she realizes it or not. I think it's generally true to say that women—no matter how individualist or ambitious they may be—still wish to marry men who will remain faithful to them, who will be able to support their families, who will be responsible and loving fathers, and who will stick by their wives into old age. To find husbands with such qualities, however, seems vastly more difficult than it did a generation ago. This is not only because there is less sexual incentive for a man to tie himself down to one woman. It's also because—as awkward as this may be for women to admit—marriage is not as good a deal for men as it used to be. A generation of wives whose prime concern in marriage is not the care of their families but the anxious protection of their autonomy has brought into being millions of relationships in which the woman is unwilling to do much for the man while expecting much in return.

During the months I spent interviewing female college students, I asked them to describe the kind of marriage (if any) they envisioned for themselves. A composite of their ideal husband went something like this: He would, foremost, recognize his wife as an equal person and treat her aspirations and desires as seriously as he would his own. He would split the household chores and child care with surgical exactitude (or, better, do more—a couple of the young women said they'd like to marry a man who stayed home with the children while they worked). He would not patronize his wife by assuming that she was too weak to look after herself in any given situation or assume that authority should fall to him because he's "the man." They also expected their ideal husband to be faithful and to be sensitive to their many moods and sexual desires. What went without saying was that the men had no right to make comparable demands upon them.

This attitude, however, has a tendency to backfire. If we are not willing to do much for our husbands, we can hardly expect them to be willing to do much for us. Sure, modern men might pitch in with the dishes or take the kids to the park more often than they used to. But the long-term surrender of their freedom, the unshrinking shouldering of the financial burdens of a family—the sacrifices they used to make in exchange for a woman's agreement to run the home—are sacrifices fewer men are willing to make. Women have gained the right to move into all spheres of society; men, from their point of view, have only lost their right to domestic comfort. Instead, they are expected to work as uncomplainingly as ever but also to clean the house, change the diapers, be constant and considerate lovers, give up the freedoms of bachelorhood, and—by the way—get their own damn tennis rackets. Boo-hoo, we women might reply. But before we shed too many crocodile tears, we might pause to consider the repercussions to ourselves.

WHEN MY mother praised the differences between her generation of husbands and mine, what she was not factoring in was the trade my contemporaries made for male compliance in marriage: male unreliability. We may have married more helpful and fair-minded husbands than our mothers or grandmothers did, but we cannot ultimately depend upon them. There's been a lot lately in the news about male irresponsibility—or, as it's sometimes called, "the male flight from responsibility." If it's not young men in inner cities recklessly impregnating teenage girls and abandoning them, then it's "deadbeat dads" skipping town on their children and support payments, or male executives trading in their aging wives for younger, more attractive models. The same impulse that leads men to sleep with women and not call them again or to date a woman for months and then vanish at the first inquiry of seriousness affects those men, too, who take the step of getting married but then blanch at any escalation of responsibility—at the suggestion of buying a house, for instance, or having a child. The sort of young man who once took it upon himself, after graduating from college, to earn a good living in order to marry and support a family has been displaced by the thirtyish single man who may earn a good and even affluent living but has no foreseeable plans to marry. This kind of man became the subject of the 1983 best-selling book, *The Peter Pan Syndrome*. We don't hear that term very much anymore, perhaps because Peter Panism is now considered less of a syndrome and more of the norm. Single women may complain that the men they meet and even live with seem immature and unwilling to settle down. But I also know married women in their thirties, eager to have children, who have confided to me that they would love to go right ahead, but they worry their husbands aren't "emotionally ready" yet to be fathers. Or they will say that they can't afford to take time out from their jobs yet to have kids. I should add that the women I've met in these situations are not especially committed to their careers—in another breath, they admit that they'd quit their jobs in a minute to have a baby. It's just that they don't think they could get by on one income.

Maybe they could, or maybe they couldn't—certainly generations of parents, as we are often reminded, got by with much less than the average couple earns today. But this isn't the point. What lies at the bottom of this attitude is a profound change in expectations, one that arises out of our egalitarian understanding of marriage: Men are no longer expected to be the sole breadwinners in their families. In fact, they no longer even feel a twinge of shame about it if they aren't. In the past, when a man married, he expected to have kids; or, rather, he didn't have much say in the matter. It would never occur to him to ask his wife to hold off until some distant and tentative point in the future. Children used to arrive as inevitably "as the rainfall," as Midge Decter once observed. Babies were not considered luxury goods. When I hear a woman say that she would like to have a baby but can't afford to leave her job, what she is really saying is that her husband is unwilling to support them if she does. And good modern wife that she is, she is embarrassed by—or feels guilty about—any hope or expectation on her part that he would.

From an equality viewpoint, this might all seem well and good. When we demanded the right to pursue the same lives as men outside the home, we were naturally obliged to give up our right to support within it. The National Organization for Women's 1969 statement of purpose put it this way: "We reject the current assumptions that a man must carry the sole burden of supporting himself, his wife, and family, and that a woman is automatically entitled to lifelong support by a man upon her marriage, or that marriage, home, and family are primarily woman's world and responsibility—hers to dominate, his to support. We believe that a true partnership between the sexes demands a different concept of marriage, an equitable sharing of the responsibilities of home and children and of the economic burdens of their support." Many women today would agree with that once provocative sentiment. In the same University of Michigan Institute for Social Research survey of high school seniors that I cited earlier, an overwhelming majority of women—70 percent—*disagreed* with the statement, "It is usually better for everyone involved if the man is the achiever outside of the home and the woman takes care of the home and family." According to the Bureau of Labor Statistics, nearly 60 percent of households with children have two breadwinners today, compared with fewer than 20 percent thirty-five years ago.

This sharing of economic responsibility, too, might appear to promote a more romantic concept of marriage, in which men and women are bound to each other by love alone, neither depending upon the other for anything but reciprocated affection. "No man should allow himself to support his wife—no matter how much she favors the idea, no matter how many centuries this domestic pattern has existed, no matter how logical the economics of the arrangement may appear, no matter how good it makes him feel," wrote former NOW president Karen DeCrow. "Love can flourish between adults only when everyone pays his or her own way." But the unfortunate discovery of my generation is that economic equality brings us no closer to "flourishing love" than the old sexual division of labor. Actually, as the divorce rate indicates, we have drifted rather further away. And this is because successful marriage has less to do with reaching equity with our husbands than it does in understanding, and accepting, the different compromises and sacrifices men and women make over the long course of marriage—compromises and sacrifices that arise out of our sexual differences, and thus our different reasons for getting married in the first place. To this degree, feminists like Simone de Beauvoir were correct: Traditional marriage did rest upon a bargain that presumed sexual disparity. But what we have discovered, in having attained such egalitarian marriages as anything de Beauvoir could have hoped for, is that this sexual disparity is *not* political in nature—arising from a "patriarchal society" determined to prevent women's equal participation in the workforce. It arises from the different roles we naturally assume when we become mothers and fathers.

It is hard to appreciate this if you don't have children, which may explain why so many of the proponents of radically egalitarian marriage have been childless, and usually unmarried—from Virginia Woolf (married, no children) and de Beauvoir (childless, never married) to Gloria Steinem, Germaine Greer, and Susan Faludi (all, at the time of writing their tomes on women, unmarried and childless). The most prominent exception to the rule is Betty Friedan, who has children but is divorced. And it is funny (if not disturbing) that these women talk about marriage as if it were some sort of theoretical domestic labor arrangement in which the tasks connected to raising children can be lumped in with other household chores. It is as if these women believe that children are nothing more than a codicil to the arrangement, an add-on option to a marriage like a leather interior and digital compass in a new car, and not the fundamental reason why men and women join together for a lifetime.

The moment you take children seriously, however, the entire dynamic changes. Your household is no longer composed of simply a man and a woman tussling over who will cook and who will clean up. The two adults suddenly find themselves at the helm of a new unit, a new team, whose success will depend upon their wholehearted commitment to each other and to their children. Whether the new arrangement is strictly "fair" to any individual within it ceases to be important, or becomes less important than whether it is "best" or "right" for the family as a whole. Over the long course of a marriage, both husband and wife will make hundreds of compromises and sacrifices for their family. At any given moment, these sacrifices and compromises may seem unduly burdensome to the person making them. The woman who stays home with her baby may feel resentful of her husband, who puts on a suit every morning and goes to a quiet office while she changes into something spit-proof and calculates whether she has enough time to take a shower before the next round of her infant's demands descends upon her. But the husband may also feel resentment of his own: that he *has* to go to a job he might not like very much, that all the cash he earns is vacuumed up by baby food, a mortgage, and payments for a car whose seats have been resurfaced with cracker crumbs and spilled formula. She envies his daytime company of adults; he envies her freedom to take a walk in the park on a summer afternoon. She feels at the mercy of the baby; he feels at the mercy of his boss and the increased pressure of his family's dependence upon him. And so it goes, all through life, each bolstering the other—in different ways but in equal measure. They will live through many things together: great joys, but also great sadness. Does it make sense to measure a person's worth in a marriage according to the amount of income he or she contributes or to get bogged down by petty power struggles over who mops and who shovels the walk?

Perversely, by encouraging men and women to strive for this sort of precise equality within marriage, we have left women and their children much more vulnerable to the whims of their husbands than ever before. The protections the law once afforded to women who made economic sacrifices for their families no longer exist. They were abolished when we rewrote the divorce law in the name of sexual equality. When a marriage breaks up, as two out of five marriages now do, a wife will seldom be entitled to alimony, no matter how much less she may earn than her ex-husband. In the 1970s, feminists campaigned against alimony on the explicit grounds that its elimination would flush women out of the home and into the workforce, where they belonged. The revocation of the old promise that marriage meant "assured support as long as they live," wrote the feminist sociologist Jessie Bernard in her 1972 book, *The Future of Marriage,*" may be one of the best things that could happen to women. It would demand that even in their early years they think in terms of life-long work histories; it would demand the achievement of autonomy. They would have to learn that marriage was not the be-all and end-all of their existence." But when women are forced to think in terms of lifelong work histories, there is a cost to be paid, and it is paid by them and their children. A divorced couple usually sells its home and divides the proceeds, after which the woman survives on what she can earn—not much if she's getting on in years and has been out of the workforce for any significant amount of time. (David Blankenhorn, author of the 1995 book, *Fatherless America: Confronting Our Most Urgent Social Problem*, estimates that the child support awarded by state courts averages only about $3,000 per year.)

Women, then, are now freer to pursue their ambitions outside the home; but by snatching away the special protections that were once afforded women who made sacrifices for their families, we have made it extremely difficult for women to do anything *but* live identical lives to men. We have, in a sense, robbed women of a choice that belonged to every previous generation of women—the choice to care for their children and expect support from their husbands for doing so.

As it is, women have not ceased to *want* to care for their children, or to be the ones in a marriage to make the financial sacrifice to do so (something I will discuss further in the next chapter): The majority of women—52 percent—still say they would prefer to be home with their children rather than working, according to a 1997 poll by Roper Starch (which has been polling women on this question since 1974). For this reason, the majority of women are not working in glamorous, high-paying, fulfilling jobs but those that offer them regular hours and flexibility: Eighty percent of working women earn less than $26,000 a year. But because of the instability of marriage today, many women feel *compelled* to keep working. They dare not take the risk of leaving their jobs lest, in ten or twenty years down the road, they find themselves divorced and in sudden need of the professional experience they might have surrendered in order to raise their children. And those women who do opt out of the workforce for their kids are frequently made to feel freakish by those around them, including their own husbands.

"My husband does not support my decision to be at home," wrote an anonymous advice seeker to a Virginia-based newsletter for at-home mothers. "He constantly makes me feel guilty about not working and often 'reminds' me that we won't be able to afford a house in our present situation. The tension isn't doing much for our marriage either. . . . Has anyone (successfully or not) dealt with this situation? I would feel better just knowing that I'm not the only at-home mother with a nonsupportive spouse." A number of readers replied to the letter with helpful rationalizations to offer her husband, including the obvious fact that it made no more sense for her to take a job that would only bring in enough to pay someone else to watch her child. But what is striking is that we even discuss this issue in such crudely economic terms—that so many women have been rendered speechless, embarrassed even, by thirty years of mockery of motherhood as it used to be. The "noneconomic" value of a wife to her husband, of a mother to her child—these are not equations that husbands used to sit down and compute when they did their bills. The value was blindingly evident, and priceless. But in order for a woman to excuse herself from the workforce and take on the nonlucrative task of raising kids and running a home, she will probably have to justify it—as much to herself as to her husband—in job-like terms. As one of the newsletter readers advised from Philadelphia: "I told my husband that my 'job' is my child. My board meeting consists of a firm but gentle reprimand explaining why a two-year-old has to hold mom's hand while crossing the street. My power lunches are trying to dole out healthy meals while making sure the whole-wheat bread does not go to the cocker spaniel. My payday is when my daughter finally walks alone down the stairs."

And it will be even tougher for a woman to take time out from her job to stay home with her kids if, before giving birth, she's been especially adamant about the fairness and equality of her marriage. Asking her husband to shoulder the whole burden of being the breadwinner will not necessarily strike him as "fair" or "equal." If she hasn't been willing to accept any of the traditional duties of a wife—indeed, if she's rejected them at every turn—how can she suddenly expect him to assume the traditional role of husband?

I once had a conversation with a man in his late thirties who had just become a father. This man viewed himself as a compassionate, politically liberal male. I'd known him to constantly champion the unfortunate against the privileged. He was deeply concerned about the potentially harsh effects of welfare reform, particularly upon single mothers. Whenever he spoke about his wife, who was, like him, a book editor for a New York publishing firm, it was always respectfully and with admiration for her talent at her job. But one day he found himself absolutely startled by her behavior. They had lived together for five years, he told me, both of them absorbed in their interesting careers. Then one day the woman, a previously reliable feminist, burst out: *"If you don't let me have a baby right away, I'm leaving. I don't care if you marry me. I just want a baby!"* Well, he married her right away and they had the baby. She thought she would go back to her job, but once their child was born, she decided she didn't want to. That was all fine with him, of course, but, he said—betraying a slight flash of resentment—things were now pretty tight and he felt a pressure on him to succeed that he hadn't before. His job, by New York standards, did not pay well and would probably never pay well. Their apartment felt too small, there would be school bills, etc., etc., and he was constantly racked with worry about how he was going to pay for it all. As he poured out his story (with a mounting sense of aggrievement), I realized that it had *never occurred* to him that he might have to provide for someone else. Here was someone who prided himself on his enlightened opinions toward women. He'd treated his girlfriend as a person utterly equal to himself. Had he done otherwise, she probably would never have involved herself with him in the first place. No wonder he felt betrayed when—lo and behold!—she suddenly and unilaterally changed the terms of their deal.

Another friend of mine, an attorney, found himself in similar circumstances after his wife, also an attorney, had a baby. He was a little more prepared to support a family—he'd eagerly wanted kids—but he wasn't prepared to support it *entirely* by himself. His wife had been reassuring on that point. Before having a baby, she'd insisted that she wouldn't want to be stuck at home with a drooling infant. She was determined to make partner one day, like him. So they bought an expensive house with a mortgage they could just manage on both salaries. They hired a full-time nanny. Then, after his wife had the baby, her feelings changed—and she decided not to go back to work. As my friend told me his story, he too expressed resentment—not so much because his wife wished to stay home, but because he'd been talked into taking on a mortgage that, if he was to meet it, would require him to work much longer than the sixty-hour work week he was already putting in. Like the man in publishing, he had believed his wife when she'd told him she would go right on working after having a child, and he felt a little foolish and hoodwinked when she didn't.

And why shouldn't he? As a modern man, he'd walked to the altar with a different understanding of marriage than had his grandfather. He knew it was no longer the old fee-for-service deal, in which he works like a dog but can expect his meals and laundry to be taken care of and a tidy, familial home to return to at the end of the day. So he'd been taught to develop other expectations. He presumed his wife would earn a good salary that would bring its compensating comforts, such as a larger house, a nicer car, and a generally more affluent life than they could afford on his salary alone. Then, after the baby arrived, everything was upended. Well, not quite everything. For while he was expected to be the sole breadwinner, he was also expected to continue to be a modern man about it, taking on his "fair share" of the household tasks when he came home at night, helping with dinner, being a great, involved dad, and making sure not to utter any word or commit any act that might be construed as "oppressive" by his wife. That he may bridle at this arrangement would be understandable. But what if he decides that it's all too much and he wants to leave?

And this is where the concept of an egalitarian marriage falters altogether. For men bridled at the arrangements of the past, too. The old deal might have gotten him a hot meal on the table and a clean house, but it could also feel confining—as much to the man, who was going to work day after day, as to the educated woman locked up in the suburbs. What made a husband get on that train every morning and stick to that marriage was a sense of obligation reinforced by those around him in the same position, and the penalties leveled against him if he left. If he decided to abandon his family for anything less than the most compelling reasons, he faced banishment from the company of respectable people as well as the obligation to support *forever* the wife and family with whom he no longer lived. The clumsy measures that were once deployed to keep men in marriage might now seem censorious or backward, but at least our society recognized that when marriages broke up, or failed to form in the first place, women and children were the ones most likely to suffer.

Today, they are still the ones most likely to suffer. Unmarried women are dramatically poorer than those who are married; and it is women, not men, who financially suffer most from divorce. And this is not because of sexism but because women still want to take primary responsibility for the care of their children. When their marriage breaks up, they nearly always want custody of their children—a costly decision. (One third of all children growing up in America today are being raised in households headed only by a mother, and one half of all kids will live in a single-parent household before they are eighteen.) There's now little disagreement, too, about the toll divorce and single parenthood take upon children. As sociologists Sarah McLanahan and Gary Sandefur discovered in their landmark 1994 study of children of single parents, children who grow up without the continuous presence of both mother and father are twice as likely to drop out of school as children raised by both biological parents. They are also more likely to become addicted to drugs and alcohol, to commit crimes, to never seek higher education, and to have more difficulty sustaining relationships. Young women who grow up without fathers are two and a half times as likely to get pregnant in their teens. One could go on and on.

Even worse, however, is the general damage done by divorce to the faith that men and women have in marriage—the fading belief in commitment, the cynicism toward love and sex, the increasingly tenuous connections to family. "My world is an upper-middle-class place with few hardships of any real kind but for the almost complete lack of familial stability," wrote a young woman named Cynthia Rutherford, a student at Harvard Business School, in an essay for her hometown newspaper. "Last January, my father's wife (three years older than I) gave birth to my first sister (correction: first *blood-related* sister). Last summer, my mother phoned me to say that she and Howard had gone to Nevada to get married (his second, her third, after seven years of living together). . . . In the same month, [my boyfriend's] mom separated from her husband (his third marriage) of two years and asked [him] to 'hide' her $8,000 engagement ring lest it be deemed community property." Rutherford went on to observe, "We are the kids of transient parents, all grown up, who run from making an emotional commitment to our girlfriends and boyfriends at all costs. To be sure, we will run in the same direction when we are parents: away from our children. It's indicative of our age that we know more parents who mail monthly child-support checks than we do those who make a point of having Sunday night dinner with their kids."

This loss of faith in marriage explains why my generation may be so zealous about making sure their marriages are so equal: A modern couple's desire to keep their arrangement strictly balanced, at all levels, is actually a way of protecting each partner's self-interest in the event that the marriage dissolves. The compromises a couple is willing to make for each other, the responsibilities the partners are willing to shoulder for their family, are bearable only if they can be assured that their marriage is going to last and that the society around them considers an enduring marriage important—indeed, worthwhile and admirable. Otherwise they may begin to feel like chumps—making sacrifices and holding themselves to certain standards of behavior that no one else they know does. A man stays in a marriage not simply because he loves his wife and children, but because he could not respect himself—or expect others to respect him—if he casually up and left, or had an affair, or brought harm to those who so deeply loved and trusted him. Likewise for a woman. She stays in a marriage and takes risks like leaving her job when the babies are born not because she finds changing diapers so intrinsically interesting or doing the laundry so fulfilling but because she feels it is right for her family. If a couple is uncertain that their marriage will last—or even that it's *important* for it to last—and each partner does not respect the sacrifices the other is making, then it will be difficult for them to make any compromises at all. They will cling to their individuality out of self-protection, constantly thinking about their own long-term self-interest, unable to think or act in terms of what is good for the family as a whole.

A couple who enters marriage with this attitude is doomed, no matter what hopeful sentiments they may express for each other at the altar.

And it's why many of the legislative efforts to shore up marriage are probably doomed as well. Some states, like Michigan, have considered repealing their "no-fault" divorce laws and reinstating alimony; others, like Louisiana and Arizona, offer those who choose it "covenant marriages," in which couples sign prenuptial contracts that would hold them to a two-year waiting period in the event they wish to divorce; and others still have suggested that couples undergo a mandatory counseling period before they marry. While the motives of these states are laudable, fines, cajolery, and therapy to keep people together are weak reeds when the force of the current is against you. Alimony helps to keep men in marriage only when they are wealthy enough to pay it: Very few men, aside from sultans and tycoons, can afford to support two households on their income, no matter how forcefully a court or government may attempt to shake more change out of their pockets. Imposing alimony will have little effect on the large numbers of middle- and working-class men who already evade paying even token amounts of child support. As for counseling and waiting periods for divorce, how can a chat with a stranger or a promise to hold off for a couple of years from seeking a divorce at the outset of a marriage help it to endure when for the rest of a married couple's lives they will receive no other indication that society takes what they're doing seriously? Some frustrated wives have resorted to the civil courts to enforce the basic marital justice that the divorce laws no longer will, like the North Carolina mother who successfully sued the "other woman" who broke up her marriage. Claiming damages under an old alienation-of-affection law, she was awarded $1 million. The victory was symbolic, though, because her husband didn't have the cash to pay her; as the sympathetic jury members explained, they simply thought it was important to "send a message" that adultery is wrong.

But perhaps a better, and more effective, way to send a message would be to change the attitude with which we now approach marriage. For despite having suffered through the highest divorce rate in the nation's history, despite the casualness with which people are often accused of seeking divorce, nearly three quarters of Americans persist in believing that "marriage is a lifelong commitment that should not be broken except under extreme circumstances." If this is true, then we have to seriously reexamine our opinions toward the so-called traditional marriage that we rejected in favor of the more egalitarian but less enduring modern one.

The many feminist critics of marriage insist that traditional marriage is incompatible with modern women's lives: that very few women would be willing to return to marriages in which the wives confine themselves largely to home and family while their husbands go to work. These critics damn any attempt to salvage, or reexamine, traditional marriage as a pointless exercise in nostalgia—when not an actively subversive attempt to "turn back the clock" on women's achievements outside the home. Indeed, feminists mistrust marriage so profoundly that their response to the harm done to women by divorce has been to urge women to avoid it entirely, and they resent all efforts to preserve it. Like disciples of Le Corbusier surveying a row of Victorian houses, they think there is nothing wrong with marriage that could not be solved by bulldozers and dynamite. As Barbara Ehrenreich wrote in *Time,* "Yes, divorce is bad—but so is the institution that generates it: marriage." Ideally, such critics believe, relationships should be formed and dissolved at whim, and there should be no assigned roles for either sex. There are thinkers, too, like Barbara Dafoe Whitehead, who recognize the harsh consequences of divorce upon women and children but who are equally reluctant to see any return to the division of labor according to sex. As she notes in the conclusion of her 1997 book, *The Divorce Culture,* "If men and women are to *find a way to share the tasks of parenthood in marriage,* that way can come about only through a change of heart and mind, a new consciousness about the meaning of commitment itself [italics mine]. . . ."

Yet this quest for perfect parity in marriage will never liberate women from our duties and cravings as mothers. What it can do—what it has done for nearly half the men in America—is provide an excuse for shirking the duties of fatherhood. If men are told they are not needed to support their wives and children, if they are made to understand that their role as father is interchangeable with the mother's—or, for that matter, with the baby-sitter's, or the day-care worker's—what compelling reason do men have to remain with their families? To open sticky jar lids and move heavy furniture? Hardly an incentive for lifelong commitment or inspiration for enduring romance. What the feminist vision of marriage amounts to is that every marriage should resemble a gay marriage, without husbands or wives or fathers or mothers. Instead, both "partners" or "spouses" should occupy the same roles within and outside the home. And all of this may sound fine, even attractive, in a science fiction sort of way, and it will last precisely as long as the romantic attraction between the two partners lasts. But what happens then? The female partner doesn't really *need* her male partner in this unisex utopia: She has her job and her day-care center and (for a while, anyway) a succession of available lovers. Nor does the male partner really *need* his female partner. He can get take-out Chinese food and (for rather longer) girlfriends and the new line of Hallmark divorced-dad cards to send to his offspring. All but the happiest marriages are held together for *reasons:* because husbands and wives seek different, supportive roles within marriage, because they rely upon each other for different things. And marriages are held together even more by *opinion*—the opinion of society that marriage is good and laudable, that separation is a calamity and a failure, and by the opinion of the husband and wife themselves that only the gravest incompatibility can justify divorce. But we have, step by step, weakened these reasons and discarded these opinions.

There is nothing now left to bind a man to his wife and children—or a wife to her husband—but the very tenuous bonds of affection and sexual attraction. If a man is decent and loves his wife and would never abandon her, well, lucky her—she's found, by today's standards, a rare gem. But what if his sense of duty and obligation are not so strong? What if he's feeling resentful or trapped or bored or sexually listless or financially overburdened? His children might be passing through some sullen and unrewarding phase, his house might be constantly messy, his wallet may feel as if it is being consumed daily by piranhas, and his wife may be cranky and tired all the time because of the pressure *she's* facing. What holds him there? Certainly not the cost of divorce—he'll be able to escape that. He will not face banishment from his church (if he goes to church), or ostracism by his friends, or disapproving looks from his neighbors, or, if he acts civilized about it, even a harsh word from his in-laws. It's not the Dark Ages, after all, he might tell himself. And then there's that smart, attractive, and, above all, *unencumbered* young woman down the hall from his office. Hey, it could be great—for *him*. He might feel guilty for a while, sure, particularly those first few weekends when the kids come around looking all mopey-eyed, but guilt is easily the most short-lived emotion, especially when the society around you tells you that you are foolish for putting up with what doesn't make you happy. For what doesn't feel right for you. For what threatens your identity as an individual. For what, above all, doesn't seem *fair*.

So how *should* women today approach marriage?

For all the scorn that has been leveled against the marriages of the 1950s, those of us who are too young to have experienced them can only read about them with a kind of awe and—dare I say it?—wistfulness. Compared to today's frantic two-career households, the suburban married life that was deemed so stifling and unfulfilling a generation ago seems blissfully peaceful and affluent. The loyal, responsible, hardworking dads of that era, long ridiculed as insensitive drones, look like pure catnip to women fed up with the inconstant, immature men of our time.

Yet the feminists are probably right in believing that very few women—and very few men—could envision themselves returning to the starkly defined roles of the past. And that's not only because these roles feel, to a modern sensibility, thwarting and unfair. It's also because it would actually make no sense today for a woman to surrender her ambitions in order to run her home and raise her children. The reason it makes no sense, however, has less to do with women's attainment of sexual equality than it does with the fact that we live in an age when we can even consider lives unhampered by our biology. Until relatively recently, no woman—unless she was very poor—would wish to face working outside the home on top of everything else. True, ironing clothes with a red-hot piece of metal and cooking meals over a wood stove was not a very attractive destiny. But coal-mining in an unventilated shaft, or pulling wheat from the ground, or riveting girders thirty storeys up was, if anything, even worse. It's no accident that the most forceful and successful push for women in the workforce occurred at the same historical moment that the birth-control pill became available, childbirth was at last safe, antibiotics and healthier diets increased the average life span, and technological advance produced hundreds of thousands of jobs that could be described as pleasant or interesting, let alone "fulfilling." Today, no woman has to be "trapped" at home and confined to her role as mother—even if, in fact, she's traditionally minded and *does* decide to take five, ten, or even twenty years out of the workforce. Not only will she emerge from the experience a more youthful and fit person than her grandmother was, with many years of life ahead of her, but the advent of personal computers and the increasing flexibility of our economy are creating jobs she will be able to do from her living room or on a part-time basis when her children start school.

Perhaps we can't have—or don't want—the marriages of the past, but that doesn't mean that the basic centuries-old principles upon which marriage was founded have ceased to apply. As Tolstoy reminds us, "If the purpose of marriage is the family, the person who wishes to have several wives or husbands may perhaps receive a great deal of pleasure, but in that case will not have a family." The different roles we assume as mothers and fathers, the different deals we wish to cut with each other in order to sustain these roles—these have persisted through thirty years of social revolution and beyond. What has not persisted is the society that recognized the mutual sacrifices husbands and wives make for each other, that understood marriage as an arrangement of give-and-take rather than quid pro quo. A woman who had been happily married for fifty-two years told a *Washington Post* reporter that when she was wed, at twenty-one, "Divorce was not an option. You know, in those days, you couldn't say cancer out loud, you said the 'Big C.' Divorce was the same thing, you said the 'Big D,' you would never discuss it. It was a disgrace in the family. When you got married, we never said, 'Well, if it doesn't work out we could always end it.' People got married and that was that. After more than a half-century of marriage, I can also tell you that it is important to realize early on that no one person can give you everything that you want or need."

Unfortunately, there is no contemporary model for a marriage in which our modern belief in sexual equality could be reconciled with the inherent differences of our sexual natures. This is why, I suppose, women are so fearful about "going back": The only alternative to the obsessively egalitarian marriage of today that they can imagine is the rejected inegalitarian one of the past. They enter into their marriages clinging to their newfound identities and newly gained territories as tenaciously as breakaway republics cling to theirs, fearful of surrendering a scrap of their independence lest the old country move in and take over again.

But it may be that in order for modern women to have the marriages we want, we will have to stop being so preoccupied about our identities, and instead develop an appreciation for the mutual, if differing, contributions we make to marriage as men and women. Maybe what we should expect from our marriages is not so much an equality in kind but an equality in spirit. We want our husbands to love and respect us, to see us as their equal in all aspects of the mind and soul, but that doesn't mean we have to do exactly the same things in our day-to-day lives or to occupy identical roles. We must also understand that family has never been about the promotion of rights but about the surrender of them—by *both* the man and the woman. A wife and husband give up their sexual freedom, their financial freedom, their right to "pursue happiness" entirely on their own terms the moment they leave the altar. No matter what may come of their marriage, they have tied their identities—and fates—together. Through the act of having children, they seal them. And this is what a woman today who takes her husband's name acknowledges with that symbolic act. She is hardly declaring herself his chattel. She is asserting, rather, that she and her husband have formed a new family, distinct from all their previous ties, both permanent and total in its commitment. It may seem arbitrary that they take the man's name instead of making up a new one or hyphenating both names like English nobles. But that is our custom, and it is by now a harmless one. (Matrilineal societies do exist, but this doesn't mean they necessarily have a superior record in the treatment-of-women department—ask the Spanish.) The husband's name, in any case, ceases to refer to just him and now reflects the combined personality of the family itself, like a newly merged corporation.

Alas, by withholding ourselves, or pieces of ourselves, instead of giving to our marriages wholeheartedly, we can't expect our husbands to do so, either. After all, it's not as if postponing marriage and going into it with our eyes more wide-open has made marriage any more stable than it was when men and women went into it practically blind. A young man I know told me that he'd "at last" moved in with his girlfriend of a few years. "We're more serious now," he said proudly. And I thought, No you're not. For marriage, as the married know, is about more than signing a lease, splitting bills, sharing chores, and professing a vague sort of long-term commitment; it's about more than being home in the evenings or spending weekends together or deciding what color to paint the walls; it's about more, even, than happiness and contentment and compatibility. It is about life and death, blood and sacrifice, about this generation and the next, and one's connection to eternity.

It is not nostalgic to wonder why this very obvious truth now seems to escape us; why so many men don't understand that it's wrong to walk out on their children and wives—or why so many women feel so nervous, so insecure, and so frightened about "losing themselves" the moment they marry. What is strange is that for so long we could be persuaded otherwise, that we could grow up mistrusting and steeling ourselves against so essential a human condition as love.

chapter four

About Motherhood

THERE IS one place to which all discussions about women eventually wind their way. On this particular evening it has ended up in the family room of a woman who has just returned home from her job as vice-president of a bank. It is not a bad commute, she says, only forty minutes. Her husband sits on the sofa, cradling their two-year-old son in his lap; he got home a couple of minutes earlier. Another son, who recently turned four, is a few feet away, trying to stand on his head while watching a Peter Rabbit video on TV. "Are you going to say hi to me?" she asks him, mockingly offended, half smiling. "Hi," he murmurs, not moving his eyes from the set even while he loses his balance and his legs flop over to the side. She loosens her blazer, idly pats her younger boy, and looks expectantly around for something. "A glass of water?" her husband offers—to which she nods. The husband passes her the child while he goes to get it. "He has an ear infection," she sighs, stroking his head. The water is brought, they chitchat a few minutes about how the boy is feeling and whether or not to take him to the doctor the next day. Then the husband pats his knees, stands, and says, "Well, I'll do bath tonight." Switching off the television, he hoists a boy over each shoulder and carries them off upstairs, from where we hear howls of protest and the sound of water running. The woman listens for a moment. When the noise seems to have settled, she leans forward and, without any preamble, begins to describe The Problem.

On some mornings, she says, "it's just awful leaving for work. My older son says, 'Mommy, I don't want you to go to work today.' He gives me a big hug, then another, then another. It's *torture*. And my younger one, he gets these big tears and watches me through the window as I go to the car. Sometimes at night, my [elder] son asks me to lie down with him on his bed, and he says, 'I'll hold your shirt so you don't go away.'

"I'm always soul-searching," she says. "You're trying to provide for a good life and that's sort of ironic. Because what is more important—the monetary aspects or being there for them?"

The dilemma that now haunts her at nearly every moment of her working day is one she never anticipated; nor had she been led to anticipate it all those years she so carefully mapped out her career. Like most women of her age and education, she'd been raised with the expectation that she'd go far in the world, that her work would be meaningful and important to her ("not just a job"). Eventually, she supposed, she'd want children, but she also assumed, when she gave it more than a moment's thought, that there would be ways to cope with them: maternity leave, day care, nannies. She rose through the bank as smoothly as her equally capable male colleagues. She worked hard and put in "face time," arriving early in the morning and leaving late at night. She didn't have to break through any "glass ceilings" or hack out new paths through the corporate jungle as her older female colleagues had been obliged to do. She met and married a man as committed to work as herself. For years she was content to absorb herself in her work, spending the little free time she had left over working out at the gym or going to dinner with her husband. Then, as she drew close to thirty, almost imperceptibly but rapidly, "my job no longer felt like enough. I think a lot of it was physiological—something goes off in the female brain, I guess, and you start thinking about kids a lot. At the same time, your career is at this momentum. You're where you worked to be and yet suddenly you have this 'little problem.' You personally don't want to wait to have kids any longer, but professionally you think maybe you should. You feel almost *treacherous* about it." And even though her boss was a working mother, she says telling her that she was pregnant "was the most difficult thing I'd ever done in my career. I just felt like I was letting her down. And that feeling, by the way, had nothing to do with what I'd thought her reaction would be. She was very good about it. So why did I feel so bad—so guilty? Where did *that* feeling come from?"

And it was only going to get worse. Before she had children of her own, she was critical of her female colleagues who did—or, at least, of those who let their families affect their work. "I was pretty insensitive," she allows. "You know, if a woman stood up at a meeting and said, 'I'm sorry, I've got to go pick up my kids,' I'd think, God, why would you say that in front of everyone?" When she herself became pregnant, she continued to believe that her return to work after maternity leave would present, at most, some scheduling problems. The thought of these didn't faze her; part of her talent as an executive was resolving such problems. And it's true that everything about her—from her tidy, short haircut to the briskness with which she walks and the precise way she gave me directions to her home—exudes mastery over her world; she is a woman who makes lists of her lists.

Every mother can see the punch line coming—or, actually, several of them at once. In the first months after a baby arrives, it seems a miracle if you can get yourself showered, let alone dressed, before six o'clock in the evening. Baby-sitters quit or aren't the Mary Poppins they seemed upon first meeting. Bosses phone and put pressure upon you to return at the same moment the baby is wailing and your husband is calling to you to find the pacifier. Your IQ, meanwhile, like the Dow on a bad day, plunges fifty points after the baby is born and doesn't rally again until he is weaned. A pleasant fog descends upon the brain; it takes three or four trips back inside before you can leave the house without forgetting something. But the toughest part—the one rather large contingency this woman, like so many, did not allow for in all her advance work—was how she would feel that first day her maternity leave was up when she placed her baby son into another woman's arms and slammed her car door to drive to the train station. How could she admit—to her boss, to her colleagues, to herself—that analyzing budget sheets was suddenly less compelling to her than reading *Hop on Pop*?

Yet neither was she willing to quit her job and stay home. As painful as she found it to leave every morning, her vision blurry from tears, her insides as heavy as wet cement, she felt she couldn't quit work. It wasn't just for the money—although that really helped things, since she and her husband had embarked upon a costly renovation of their house. But the main reason, she says, was she just didn't know *who she was* or *what she would be* without her job. For while her work may have lost some of its luster, the title on her business card contributed as much to her sense of her identity as being a mother (and maybe more so). "I can't imagine myself not having an outlet," she says, glancing toward the stairs as the muffled cries of one of her sons are soothed by her husband. "I'd ask myself, Do I really want to give all of that up?" She liked putting on a grown-up suit in the morning instead of the mom's uniform of sweatshirt, jeans, and running shoes. She liked reading the newspapers and drinking her first cup of coffee undisturbed in the mausoleum silence of her office. And when her brain began to throb a little from the worry and guilt and pain of leaving every day, she'd remind herself that her baby was in good, capable hands and that there would come a day very soon when she wouldn't want to be one of those mothers living through her children long after her children had ceased to live through her.

She found her maternal substitute in an older woman who replied to a classified ad she'd placed for a full-time nanny. This woman is *terrific*, she tells me—just *adores* the boys. She decided to hire her, in fact, over the phone. The elder woman had said, after making the appointment to meet, "Whoever you hire, dear, just make sure she loves your children." The nanny was a little older than she expected—in her sixties—but the comment had rung so nicely in her ears that she traded the woman's warmth for the energy to keep up with two small boys. They don't get out as much as she'd like—you know, to the park, for walks, the mother acknowledges—but they are with someone she trusts, and it eases her conscience to know that they are getting affection in her absence. Yet even the comfort of finding such help, she admits, did not solve the other crushing, daily burden of being a working mother: the sheer shortage of time to meet demands. "I'm efficient. I can juggle *a lot* of balls in the air," she says wearily. "But it now feels like *everyone* wants a piece of me—my children, my husband, my boss, my staff. There is *no time* for anything else. Sometimes my husband and I don't even talk in the evenings. We're too tired of dealing with people all day. Sometimes if there is something important to talk about, we agree to talk about it later. During the week we're out of commission entirely. We don't see friends anymore. . . ."

As she speaks, still sipping a glass of water, the newly finished kitchen, just off the family room where we sit comes into focus behind her. This is for what they'd endured so many months of "construction craziness" and spent so much money fixing up: polished mahogany cabinets, a chef's island, a stainless-steel fridge that could hold an entire dismembered cow but at this moment holds little more than a few tins of apple juice and the congealed remains of a take-out pizza.

"Do you get time to cook?" I ask her.

She shrugs. "I eat or I don't eat. The nanny feeds the kids most nights, before we get home. Maybe I'll have a bowl of popcorn, or we'll order in. Some evenings I work after the kids go to bed. As a rule, I try to do that very little. If I have to, though, I do.

"And then there's just getting the ordinary stuff done. Tomorrow I'm doing a presentation. It will end at two P.M. and it's out here [in the suburbs] near my house. I can leave for the day after it's over. So do I (a) come home because it's precious time to have with the kids, or (b) go back to the office to clean up some stuff I haven't had time to do—or do I maybe do (b) then (a), because I could still be home early, or do I finish some errands or maybe go to Wal-Mart later with the kids because it's open until eleven?"

Her husband comes downstairs from putting the kids to bed and overhears this last sentence. "But [our younger son] is sick—"

"But he is sick," she repeats mechanically, nodding. "So I guess I'll be home early."

"Like *I* was today," he adds.

She reacts as if she didn't hear him, and maybe she didn't because she's staring dreamily into the carpet, looking like she's still tallying up the next day's tasks. Although he appears to be the most helpful of fathers, it's *she* who feels at the mercy of the children's demands, she tells me, after he's left the room again. If anything goes wrong, no matter how minor—if the sitter calls in sick or the dishwasher backs up or, as with her son this evening, a fever develops and they need to get a child to the doctor to have his ears peered into—her whole carefully balanced structure collapses. She relates this without any air of aggrievement: She clearly approves of the arrangement, and says she would not like it any other way, coming home to a husband in an apron, for instance, an idea that makes her face crinkle up in disgust. Taking responsibility for the household's day-to-day demands is the one way she may differentiate her role as mother from his as father, that she may prove to herself, and to them, that she is needed for different things, emotional things, and can be relied upon to provide them. Still, it's tough. I often think that the modern working mother's life resembles the ancient Hindu theory that the entire world rests upon the back of a gigantic turtle. It may seem bizarre that something so huge and precarious can balance upon something as insignificant, say, as a plumber's appointment, but there it is.

"And then the kids," she continues. "You wonder sometimes if they act up more because you're not around. I've talked about this with my colleagues. Have you ever noticed that the kids of mothers who stay at home tend to be better behaved?"

It may be true, or it may not be. But when you're not around your kids much during the day, you lose touch with the rhythms of their behavior. Unless a kid starts suddenly beating up other kids at preschool or throwing tantrums all the time, it is hard to judge what is naughtiness-as-usual and what is a reaction to your absence. And then the days you do spend entirely with them are jarring: When your whole week is adjusted to the sober FM atmosphere of an office, tuning it back to the screaming talk-radio station of toddler life is nerve-rattling. These mismatched environments, and the pull and push between them, make the banker feel that she is never fully part of either. When she speaks about the women she knows who quit their jobs, it's with a mix of envy and panic, masked by contempt. "A lot of them lose interest in everything *but* their children," she says dismissively. "They can't talk about anything else."

On the other hand neither, really, can she. And this is maybe the ultimate irony of her situation: She has gone to work in large part to be free of domestic worries but she is no less consumed by them, even at a distance, encased in her glass tower. At one point, she went through her company's employee directory counting up how many of the female executives had children and how many did not (about half). Knowing this didn't solve anything for her. At another point she considered going part-time, an option her company officially supports. But part-time at her job-level, she says, usually means "you get paid half-time but work full-time." No one—male or female—can defy a corporate culture, or any profession for that matter, that requires the full efforts of all its employees. As she concedes, she couldn't do her job part-time anyway, even if the company were run by Dr. Spock. "The environment changes so rapidly these days that it's difficult to keep up part-time. I'd lose ground."

And so when she gathers with other working mothers, their conversation invariably falls back on The Problem: Do you quit or keep working? They form something of a secret agony society around the water cooler, she chuckles, regaling each other with horror stories of the nanny quitting/the nanny stealing/the phone call from the emergency room. They gulp down every detail of trials that involve abusive or murderous babysitters. They pore over every news story about studies that purport to show whether day care is good or harmful to kids. They constantly prod and investigate how the other mothers are "managing," as if one of them might have stumbled upon a miracle drug that will zap guilt and stress. And it is the banker who will now brazenly announce to the expressionless faces around the boardroom table that she's got to go because of her kids. It's important to do that, she insists, so that everyone understands that family commitments are real and nothing to be ashamed of; it's not like sneaking out to play a round of golf. But these plucky little announcements are also her *only* acknowledgment to the company of the pressure upon her which is so crushing that it sometimes makes her head feel as if it is going to implode on the train home from work.

As MODERN women, we are taught to anticipate many things in our lives—except one. Like the banker, we may plot every move of our advancing career as carefully and thoughtfully as a cartographer. But the single most profound, life-changing decision that the majority of us eventually make is the one we are now least prepared for—the act of having a child. This is why all discussions of what we will do and how we will choose to live our lives invariably circle back to this one "problem." The received wisdom of our time has been to be wary of motherhood—to "fit it into" our careers and to "do it when it's convenient" and "to not let it define you." The discovery when we do have babies, of course, is that they in no way "fit into" *any* career, that they can never be described as "convenient," and that motherhood is about as defining an experience as any human being can undergo.

This is maybe the greatest surprise upon becoming a mother. Before you have a child, and even while you are pregnant, you anticipate a certain period of mayhem immediately following the baby's birth: nights without sleep, feedings, unstoppable crying, etc. That much is familiar from Hollywood comedies. But what isn't familiar, especially to women raised to believe in the importance of their work, is just how much a child will dominate a mother's mind. The woman with a slightly enlarged belly who announces that she plans to return to her office six weeks/six months/two years after her baby is born may genuinely believe she will be able to do so—and in many cases, she will do so. But what she is also revealing is how little she really knows about what is about to wallop her, hard. For until you are holding your actual baby in your arms—the baby you think looks *exactly* like you if you were a bald Martian—and marveling at the curve of his ear and his unearthly bright eyes that squint at you with astonishment and curiosity, you can't know how you're going to feel when you become a mother. This surprise is motherhood's greatest joy and its darkest secret: Suddenly, you can't stop thinking about your child. You don't stop even when you're doing something important, like being president of a bank, or something distracting, like watching a movie. All that happens is that a dimmer switch inside you turns down a little, enough for you to concentrate on something else. But it never goes out completely.

It's strange, then, that in all the public discussions of the problems faced by working mothers, the most animating aspect of motherhood—that we love our children more than anything else and want to be with them as much as we possibly can—goes unmentioned. This is not because it is an obvious fact of nature that everyone takes for granted. Rather, if you believe even modestly in women's equality, it's a fact that is too explosive to confront. For more than thirty years the women's movement has told us that we would be happier, more fulfilled human beings if we left our homes and children and went out to work. To the degree that we might feel misgivings or guilt about leaving our babies to others to raise, we have been assured that such feelings are imposed upon us by society, and sexist—no more normal for a mother to experience than a father. Instead, we've been taught to suppress these worries and to put our work ahead of our families, or at the very least, to attempt to "balance" the demands of boss and baby. Any strong rush of maternal feeling, any desire to surrender pieces of our professional selves, is viewed as a reversion to some stereotype of motherhood the women's movement was supposed to have emancipated us from. The popular books on motherhood being written by feminists today are no less vehement than they were in 1972 that full-time motherhood is a servile and ultimately dangerous state for women to succumb to. Being a good mother, they say, means taking care of ourselves first and learning to let others' needs come second. The so-called "Good Mother," who makes sacrifices for her children, has been "again and again, the means of restricting women's worlds and prohibiting them from engaging equally in the public world of men," writes Diane Eyer in her 1996 book, *Motherguilt: How Our Culture Blames Mothers for What's Wrong with Society.* (Eyer is also the author of the 1993 book, *Mother-Infant Bonding: A Scientific Fiction.* Is it important to mention that this great authority on maternal feeling is not a mother?) Not only this, but women are often told it is actually *better* for a mother to work outside the home, because she will be more satisfied that way and she will foster in her children a much healthier sense of independence. Mothers "*should* work outside the home. If they do not, they cannot preserve their identities or raise children," Joan K. Peters argues in *When Mothers Work: Loving Our Children Without Sacrificing Our Selves* (1997). "Sacrifice has no place in the motherhood pantheon," declares Susan Chira in her 1998 book, *A Mother's Place: Taking the Debate About Working Mothers Beyond Guilt and Blame.* "As I and many other mothers and their children have found, our bonds can survive hours or days apart . . ."

And in this, the women's movement has been spectacularly persuasive. The mother who does not work outside her home has become a social and statistical novelty: Sixty-five percent of mothers of preschool children now work for wages. For a working mother to admit to her desire to be with her children—or, worse, to say she'd *rather* be with them than at the office—is to question the continuing exhaustive efforts to make women equal to men in the workforce; and not just equal in pay but, as the goal now is, equal in the hours they work, in the titles they hold, in the power they wield, and in the proportion they make up of any given occupation, whether it's fire fighting or plumbing. Whenever a news report is broadcast about women's "gains" and "losses," this is the presumption that underlies it: Women are seen to have *gained* in equality when they near statistical parity with men in some realm of life (for instance, if they were to account for two hundred of the Forbes 400), and to have suffered *losses* when, for example, the number of female executives drops in a given year. Yet we should realize that in order to achieve such a level of parity, *all* women would have to work *all* of the time, whether they are the mothers of small children or not.

That women—and in particular, mothers—might not desire this version of equality is not something those tallying up our successes in tidy statistical columns wish to consider. This isn't to say that mothers must entirely abandon their work or careers in order to have children. But it *is* to say, no matter how much we might pretend or wish it otherwise, that having babies affects and constrains even the most ambitious among us, and affects and constrains us differently from men. Indeed, women's tendency to interrupt their careers for their children, or to take less demanding and less lucrative jobs, is the main cause of the notorious pay gap between the sexes. June O'Neill, head of the Congressional Budget Office, pointed out in her definitive report on the wage gap that women aged twenty-seven to thirty-three earn 98 percent as much as men of similar education and work experience. It is only *after* they become mothers, O'Neill concludes, that the priorities and career paths of women simply change.

So long as we continue to deny this, both publicly and to ourselves, all we do is exacerbate the guilty tension that is felt by every working mother at nearly every moment of her working day. This tension grips her around her leg when she leaves in the morning and hurls itself at her when she comes back through the door in the evening. It places a question mark next to every appointment she jots down in her Filofax. It's the reason she calls home six times a day—or not at all. This maternal tension is now a cliché, a staple part of any magazine feature on the problems of modern women, although it's usually spoken of as mere physical stress, the side effect of the busy, productive lives we lead—the implication being that if we could only organize ourselves better, or get dads to help out more, or magically squeeze more minutes out of each day, it would go away. But the tension is, as mothers know, not due to a simple shortage of hours. Rather, it's an *existential* lack of time, a feeling of constantly being pulled, as the banker described it, between two highly pressured worlds.

A friend of mine, recalling a period in her life when she was the single mother of two young children and also held down a full-time job, said on most days she felt like the "spinning plate" act on the old *Ed Sullivan Show:* She was constantly running back and forth, trying not to let any of the spinning plates she was balancing fall to the ground and smash. You don't have to be a single mother to experience this. When I became a mother, I found that I'd unwittingly joined something akin to a secret corps of women, all of us engaged in the same day-to-day spinning-plate operation. Our eyes seek each other out in crowded restaurants, supermarket lines, airplanes, and rush-hour trains. We will help a stranger distract her children while she fishes in her purse for tissues or change. We hold open doors for each other and sigh sympathetically when everything seems to go embarrassingly wrong at once: a child wails, a package drops, a cashier taps her pen impatiently. "Here, let me help you" are usually the opening words between two mothers in public, and it's inevitably funny, because the other mother is nearly always as saddled down with packages and strollers and babies as you are—it's just that she's got them momentarily under better control. Stony-faced strangers, hands completely free, will either pass by with irritation or remain dreamily oblivious. And this is just *basic* motherhood.

Working, even at a part-time job, is the equivalent of a clown tossing three more spinning plates onto a stick balanced precariously on the end of a mother's nose. Suddenly, it doesn't take much to make her drop one—a note, for instance, that comes home with her child from school asking her to send in a shoe box on Thursday for an art project. It wouldn't have been so bad if the teacher hadn't also sent home a note earlier that week reminding her to put her child in his school shirt on Wednesday because the class is going on a field trip, and also to remember to pack extra sandwiches on Friday for the homeless delivery and, by the way, to please sign the volunteer sheet for the upcoming school fair at which every parent is expected to do *something*. Then there is the completely different schedule of another child (if she has another one, or two . . .) to keep in her head, on top of the regular routine of after-school classes, play dates, team practices, and car pools. This also doesn't count the additional tasks of running a household, the chores, laundry, and cooking (even if it's frozen or take-out most nights). When you factor in a job on top of all of this, it's no wonder you see so many women sitting on subway cars at five-thirty looking absolutely stupefied, staring into the middle space of the floor, unable to summon enough energy to read a newspaper while their bodies are hurtled from one arena of demands to another.

When you speak to mothers about this madness, they usually accept it as the inevitable price of working. Like the banker, they believe the only way to cure it is for a woman to quit her job outright, which for some is not possible and for many would be unacceptable. Yet whether you work because you want to or because you have to, the outcome for women is the same—the nagging, underlying worry that what you are doing is hurting those you love most. And this is especially hard upon those women who, unlike the banker, leave their babies every day to work at jobs they don't even have the consolation of finding fulfilling.

Another woman I met, who works in the customer service division of a large department store chain near Niagara Falls, New York, suffers all the exhaustion and internal bleeding of the working mother's existence but, unlike the banker, would quit her job tomorrow if she won the lottery. For her, it seems a little inane to talk about career satisfaction: Her job consists of angry customers calling her up seven hours a day complaining that the Dustbuster they bought was faulty and demanding to know what she's going to do about it. Given the choice, she'd rather be at home, eating lunch with her twin daughters. But she can't afford that. So, like the banker and her colleagues, she is trying to find some "medium cure" that will help ease the pressure, and for that reason she signed up for a morning-long "stress workshop" sponsored by her company—a growing trend in the corporate world for exhausted employees. This one is held in a hotel conference room about a mile down the highway from where she works.

The program is taught by a fortyish "stress expert" named Mary, who would qualify as a candidate herself for the workshop if she were not already running it. A thin, nervous-looking woman, Mary displays the weariness of someone who is always in motion but cannot cease. When I first interviewed her in her office at a hospital clinic, her phone was ringing every few seconds while her computer flashed arrivals of E-mail. Her pager sounded in mid-conversation, and it took her a few moments of rustling through her big, overstuffed leather bag to find it and switch it off. She called her workshop "The Struggle to Juggle," but sometimes she got mixed up and referred to it, more aptly, as "The Juggle to Struggle."

About forty employees of the department store chain, mostly women but with a sprinkling of men, show up for her morning workshop. They sit at chairs behind long tables, wearing the expectant but somewhat skeptical expressions of a village audience about to watch a demonstration of magic potions by a traveling salesman. The abstract strains of recorded New Age music waft through the room. Slides appear on an overhead projector screen: "Wellness is . . . integrating body, mind, and spirit to impact on your state of health"; "Stress is . . . the arousal of body and mind in response to demands made upon them (stressor/perception/response)"; "Agenda: Listen to your body." The phrases are comforting in a clinical way: The madness of our lives can be managed like our diets. Mary begins by announcing to the room, "I'm not coping. I have two teenage girls and an eight-year-old son. I'm enrolled in a fellowship program three evenings a week. But this is a *choice* I'm making. There is no magic fairy dust that will make you stress-free."

The participants' faces remain neutral through this personal revelation, politely so. They don't visibly react until Mary tells them a story about her white floors. She had them installed in the downstairs of her house six months ago. Wasn't that stupid? she says. Now, on top of everything else, she has floors she can never keep clean. Every time she walks across them, she notices a footprint or a scuff that she knows she will never get the chance to wipe away. The women in the room nod; a few giggle. Then they begin to open up—standing, introducing themselves briefly by their department or position ("Tracy, bill collection," "Anna, I'm a secretary") and then launching into similar tales of domestic chaos. It's quickly apparent that these women not only feel that they don't have enough time—they don't have enough *life*. And to the degree that they do, it's out of control.

"When I'm home, I'm always getting negative with my kids and husband."

"I say all the time: When will I get time to myself? *When?*"

"I feel a lot like I'm on an assembly line, and sometimes it speeds up."

Mary listens sympathetically and responds with more of her stress maxims. "We need to give ourselves permission to admit our imperfections to each other." "We're going to have to be smarter about the way we do things. Stress is part of life. It's what keeps us alive."

As the participants file out, not visibly consoled, Mary gives them each a "goal setting" chart. One woman mumbles, "My goal is to get wealthy and quit my job." Mary doesn't hear her. She advises people to hang their goal lists prominently in their houses, on the fridge or the bathroom cabinet, and look at it often. "You've got to take care of yourselves," she adds. "You're worth it."

Back home in her kitchen, the woman from customer service says that she was pretty disappointed with the stress workshop. After all, taking an herbal bath once a week and reminding herself of all the goals she isn't achieving won't drive away the feeling that she isn't doing what is best for her family, even though it's the best she can do. She broods as much as the banker about quitting her job or about finding some sort of flextime arrangement, but she feels boxed in because any change in her job would threaten the benefits she has accumulated over sixteen years of working for the same company. It had taken a long time for her to have kids. When she gave birth to twin girls, at the age of thirty-six, she called them her "miracle babies." Her daughters were born prematurely and "they basically didn't sleep for five years. They were so small that they got into the habit of never sleeping well. Even when they were four, they'd wake up five and six times a night." She took six months' maternity leave and, dreading going back to work, extended it for another month without pay. But her return couldn't be postponed indefinitely, and when she began her job again, "for a few years I was a total zombie. Me and my husband—we were totally exhausted. When I'd found out I was pregnant, I said I'd never complain—but I'd never been so tired! I thought to myself, There is a God, because I don't know how else I got through it."

Her husband worked rotating shifts at a steel mill. Some weeks he was around during the day to look after the babies; other weeks, they relied on a series of temporary baby-sitters. She was constantly worrying about her daughters, and constantly feeling guilty about leaving them. When the girls were old enough for preschool, she paid extra to put them in a full-day program so they could stay in one place instead of being shuttled around by sitters. It cost nearly as much as she earned to do so, but she justified this by reminding herself she was hanging on to her benefits—if she dropped out or went part-time, she'd lose those. And she worried she'd risk never being rehired full-time again. Now that her daughters have reached kindergarten, the pressure has eased up on her a bit, although she says she still "doesn't sit down until about eleven at night. I don't have time to read a newspaper. I haven't read anything since the twins were born." And while she still lives in the town in which she was raised, near her four brothers and sisters, she doesn't receive any help from her family. "My sisters and sisters-in-law all work, too." She shrugs. "Everyone is too busy, into their own lives. . . ."

With this comment, she acknowledges, without resentment, one of the starkest changes that has taken place between this generation of women and the last. Like the supermalls that paved over rows of shops, the move of women into the workforce leveled the traditional community of support. The neighborhoods have emptied of families during the day; the swings in the local playgrounds are pushed by nannies and baby-sitters; schools no longer send children home for lunch; day-care facilities have replaced the dining halls and craft centers of church basements. The nineteenth-century feminist Charlotte Perkins Gilman once predicted, "The home of the future is one in which not one stroke of work shall be done except by professional people who are paid by the hour." Walk through any middle-class neighborhood at two o'clock in the afternoon and you'll see darkened windows and maybe the figure of a cleaning lady vacuuming or taking out the garbage, but the houses and the streets will be silent except for the twitter of birds and the occasional wailing siren. When she was growing up, the woman continues, "There were always aunts and uncles and cousins around. My sister and I, we helped my mother." Her father was a plumber and electrician; her mother raised their five children. They paid for it by being thrifty. The bungalow she grew up in measured, at most, six hundred square feet. There weren't after-school activities for the kids—there were chores.

Her demands, she concedes, are higher than her parents'. She and her husband bought the 1990s equivalent of a 1960s split-level—a custom-built neo-Colonial in a suburban cul-de-sac. The bungalow she grew up in would fit neatly into their living room. They have a double garage with two cars to fill it, a kitchen with every appliance, a television that dominates the entire wall opposite their sofa. Her girls, she says, "have almost everything on the market—clothes, toys. They take gymnastics, skating, swimming. . . ." And as she tells me more about her life, it becomes clear that she didn't hang on to her job, despite all the exhaustion and guilt, simply to keep her benefits. "If I quit," she says, "we'd keep our home. But we'd have to go back to the days of my growing up—no extras. We wouldn't think of doing fun things anymore. We'd have to give up some of the kids' activities, end the restaurants and the take-out food." As it is, the twins own so many Barbies that it takes her an hour to clean them up and organize them. "All those little shoes. . . ." she sighs.

Yet she admits that achieving this material comfort is not much consolation if she has little time to enjoy it. She is no less at the mercy of other people's demands upon her than her housewife mother was—it's just that "other people" now include a boss, colleagues, day-care workers, and baby-sitters, on top of everyone else. And in this sense, women have come full circle, back to experiencing the busy but spiritually empty lives from which we hoped work would emancipate us.

My generation was raised to believe that by providing for our children's physical and material needs, we could compensate for the maternal comfort they lost by having us at work. Just so long as they were in "good care," we were told, we wouldn't have to worry about compromising our career. But this has proven to be a chimera: No amount of Fisher-Price geegaws, cheerfully painted walls, and chirping, brisk day-care workers and nannies can replace a mother's love and attention. Nor can putting our children in these surroundings ease our maternal fears for their well-being and our aching for their company. Yet on the surface of things, and given the fervor with which women have been urged into the workforce, it's no wonder women are inclined to doubt their feelings of guilt and worry. The day-care center/baby-sitter seems *fine*. I *need* to go to work.

Why does this all have to be so upsetting? And it's true that you could look at the relatively affluent lives of women like the banker and the customer service worker and wonder, What are they complaining about, given all that they have? Especially since these women, unlike single mothers, at least have husbands around to help them. But then such a reaction only underscores this perfect circle we've come from Betty Friedan's day, when women who weren't working but lived in similarly affluent suburban circumstances were chastised for not being content given all that they had. The lesson is, if you're living your life unhappily, it's certainly better to be doing so in comfortable surroundings—but those comfortable surroundings will not prevent you from being unhappy. Telling working mothers that they are wrong to feel guilt and stress and unhappiness won't make them feel better; it will simply make them feel *worse* about themselves for having these feelings, and more confused as to why they're having them in the first place. The working mothers who attend office-sponsored stress seminars or take up aromatherapy and meditative programs that teach them to "let go" are the modern-day equivalent of the depressed housewives of a generation ago, who were criticized for not being able to manage their boredom or take enough satisfaction in doing the laundry and who eventually found their way into therapy and lithium addiction. In all the breaking down of barriers we've done over a generation, this last remaining barrier—our love for our children—is the stubborn one we haven't been able to push through.

Instead, we've gotten into the perverse, schizophrenic habit of speaking about motherhood as if it were an identity that could be put on and taken off like a change of clothes: From nine to five I'm a worker, in the evenings I become a mother, and when I get up in the morning, I'm a worker again. We've had to nag fathers to behave more like mothers, demanding that they take a bigger share in the diaper changing and child minding, only to discover that when they do, it's still not enough. And to our colleagues and bosses, we've had to pretend that really nothing could be further from our minds than attending our daughter's school play when there are so many more important—and did we mention interesting?—tasks to be handled at work, tasks that will take until eight in the evening to finish. The same friend of mine who used the spinning plate analogy to describe her life also told me about a Christmas Eve she spent at work, writing a newsletter her boss insisted get finished that night. She said it nearly broke her heart thinking about her two little kids waiting for her to come home while she labored like some modern-day Bob Cratchit over the cheerless jargon of a routine corporate report. (The report, of course, was forgotten by the next week, but her children to this day remember the Christmas Eve their mother didn't come home.) When Brenda Barnes, one of the highest-ranking female executives in the United States, resigned from her job as CEO of Pepsi-Cola North America in September 1997, she'd come to a similar conclusion about the value of her work. She made the decision, she told the press, when one of her children said it would be okay to keep working if Barnes could "promise to be at home for all our birthdays." A male entrepreneur, commenting on Barnes's resignation in *The Wall Street Journal,* observed, "The truth is, no one wants to say it or print it, but a lot of these jobs are crap and a lot of these demands are just awful. One day you come in after your latest trip on the red-eye, beat to crap, and you say, 'I just don't want this stuff anymore.' "

So it's with some defensiveness that the same advocates who promised that work would be a panacea for women now claim that if it's not, the blame belongs to a society unwilling to provide adequate child care. If we had government-funded, high-quality day care, the conventional argument goes, women would no longer be hampered by the demands of their children and could fully realize their potential as citizens and workers. It doesn't seem to matter that parents have shown a marked aversion to the sort of institutional day care these advocates wish to foist upon them: Only 1.8 million of the 10 million children under five whose mothers work are in institutional care (the majority are minded by fathers, grandparents, and other relatives). Nor does it seem to matter that a careful reading of the very sketchy research on children put in day care leaves in place the common sense conclusion that nonfamily care of very young children tends to be damaging. As Dr. Diane Fisher, a clinical psychologist and authority on child development, has observed, "No matter how high-quality the day-care center is, the children still take their naps in little rows of mats on the floor, children still sit in the corner sucking their thumbs and waiting for mommy." The call for "universal child care" has become a mantra among women's groups, a cure-all, and the yardstick by which they judge any politician's commitment to women's equality.

But while the problem of child care is very real, and often a nightmare, for working mothers, it's not essentially The Problem. The Department of Health and Human Services could announce tomorrow that it is creating a system of completely free day-care centers, each one headed by Mary Poppins, and The Problem wouldn't go away. For despite all the re-assurances to the contrary, the woman who kisses her child's forehead each morning before walking out the door to her office still harbors the agonizing suspicion that what her child needs most is *her*. And the so-called solutions that are constantly being advocated in the name of working mothers—whether it is better child care or family-leave acts that allow parents time off to go to the dentist with their kids—merely aggravate The Problem, because they are based upon the wrong assumption: that a mother wants and needs more help being in the workforce away from her children, not less.

Feminists tend to react angrily to this sentiment. It is odious, they say, to insist that mothers should be the ones who sacrifice their work for their children, and not fathers equally. It is disturbingly sexist to say that women are "better" at caring for infants, or more suited to it, than men. And anyway, feminists will argue, the issue is moot, because even if most women wanted to, they couldn't afford to stay home with their kids and it's elitist to suggest that they should. As many critics said about Brenda Barnes at the time, and indeed about other prominent women before her who gave up lucrative careers for their families (such as *New York Times* columnist Anna Quindlen), isn't it nice they have the "luxury" and "choice" of doing so.

But the question we ought to be asking is why, in the space of a generation, we have come to consider taking care of our own kids—even if it's just for the few short years before they are in school—as a perk of the rich, like yachting? This was not true even in the depths of the Great Depression. It *is* true that working- and middle-class women have always done work of some kind—whether it was voluntary or part-time or from their homes. It is strange however that in the *richest* period *ever* in our history we should suddenly be considering a massive federal program to care for infants because the majority of mothers feel they have "no choice" but to work.

Part of the reason for that perception of lack of choice is the burden of taxes an average family is expected to shoulder today compared to a generation ago and the penalties in our tax code that make it more costly for one parent to stay home. But even allowing for this greater tax burden, there are many women working who, from a financial standpoint, don't strictly *have* to, whose incomes in fact just cover the cost of their child care. My generation is accused—justly, I think—of having higher expectations for our standard of living than our parents or grandparents did. My mother likes to remind me of how little she and my father got by on when my brother and I were babies. It's a perk of age, I suppose, to be able to talk about how much harder times were in the past. In my mother's case, it is certainly true. We lived in a tiny, sparsely furnished apartment. My father, who was handy with things, constructed coffee and end tables out of boards and bricks. We didn't own a car, and in the winter my mother pulled us to the grocery store upon a sled! ("Were you barefoot, too?" I tease her.) Today, the average house is larger and better, products like TV sets, stereos, and furniture are cheaper, and fresh food is more widely available. Conservatives lambast parents who put their children in day care and then buy a second car as selfish yuppies, willing to put their material needs ahead of their children. Still, extravagance and selfishness are not new human traits. Yes, we expect a lot more material comfort nowadays, and there are parents who achieve affluence by sacrificing their children. But I don't believe placing a baby in day care is either easily or thoughtlessly done by most mothers.

No, the fundamental reason why mothers of small children feel they cannot afford to stay home today, when a generation ago they didn't, is the greater prospect of divorce. The modern woman expects to support herself, and knows the danger of being unable to do so. The fear a woman has of having to fend for herself and her children at some point underlies why even happily married women often feel obliged to work when there's no immediate financial reason for them to do so. If a woman could be *sure* that her husband would stay with her, the cost of leaving the workforce might well be bearable. She might in that case tell herself, Well, *my* income if I return to work won't be as high as it might have been, but the two of us will earn enough together, and we'll share the satisfaction of knowing that our kids were cared for properly. But because no woman today can be sure, she must make her life choices defensively, staying in the workforce—even though she might not want to, even though she could afford to leave it—to protect herself in case of divorce. Combine the women who must work because they are single mothers and the women who feel they should work to protect themselves lest they become single mothers, and you realize that what looks like a child-care crisis is really a symptom of America's larger marriage crisis.

Okay, feminist critics may still fairly argue, even if we all went back to the traditional marriages of the 1950s, even if we could mitigate the need to work, women would still *want* to work. That's why those seemingly idyllic marriages broke apart. Very few women would be content to remain angels of the houses. And that's true to some degree, too. But then the question we might want to ask ourselves is how can we arrange our work better around the lives of our children instead of vice versa. Simply saying that women *want* to work does not excuse *preferring* to work after we've brought an infant into the world. Arlie Russell Hochschild wrote in her 1997 book, *The Time Bind*, of parents who "flee the pressures of home for the relief of work." These working mothers found it pleasanter, less menial, and more fulfilling to be at the office than stuck at home with their infants. But, really, what sort of argument is that? No one compels us to have babies. When we do bear them, we have an obligation to care for them, no matter how dull and tiring it may be. The local Humane Society will not let you adopt a puppy if you work full-time. Why should our standards for children be any less? Yet the feminist wisdom has been that the child should always be the *first* spinning plate a woman drops, even if it's the one most precious to her. She must *never* let go of any of the ones to do with her work. But if you're going to work and have children, some piece of your life inevitably has to give. As a startled broadcasting consultant quipped to *The Wall Street Journal* in the wake of Brenda Barnes's resignation, "What state is our society in that deciding to take care of your kids is headline news?"

All right then, the same feminists may go on to argue, why should it be *women* who must make the sacrifice and not men? But this question only makes sense if you believe there is no innate or important difference between mothers and fathers—that we are, or should be, biologically interchangeable; our roles as parents, androgynous. The fact is, when children come along, *someone* has to accommodate them. A woman who has carried the baby around for nine months inside of her usually finds it natural to do so—and often impossible not to. Some may prefer, for ideological reasons, to switch the job to the man. Supreme Court Justice Ruth Bader Ginsburg once told a newspaper reporter that she'd readily consented to a flexible schedule for one of her male clerks so he could care for his children while his wife worked at a demanding job as an economist. "This is my dream of the way the world should be," she said. "When fathers take equal responsibility for the care of their children, that's when women will be truly liberated." Except in this instance the father wasn't taking *equal* responsibility; he was taking *most* of the responsibility—as one parent of small children must if the other is going to work full-time. If a father is willing to do that, well, *swell*. But in most cases it is still women who not only adjust or sacrifice their work to their families, as June O'Neill found, but in poll after poll express the desire to do so. For all the feminist insistence that the world of *Ozzie and Harriet* is dead, the truth is that *women themselves* wish to stay home with their children if they possibly can. Only about one third of the 7.2 million married women with children younger than three work full-time. The 1997 Roper Starch poll of women's attitudes toward work found that a majority of married women would prefer to stay home with their young children if they could—and that this majority has been growing since 1985. Interestingly, there is also agreement among working and nonworking women about the effect of working mothers on society as a whole: When a 1997 NBC News/*Wall Street Journal* poll asked whether more mothers working outside the home was a step in the right direction for American society, a step in the wrong direction, or something that would make a difference, 40 percent of women employed full-time, 40 percent of women employed part-time, and 42 percent of mothers who weren't working outside the home said the trend was a bad one. Barely three in ten of all respondents (male and female) thought the trend was a step in the right direction.

And this makes sense. For the younger generation of women, work is stripped of the novelty and glamour it once held. Women (like men, for that matter) who can be described as having interesting, fulfilling jobs represent a tiny minority of the workforce. There are about 100,000 female lawyers in America. More than 600,000 women work as receptionists, more than 1 million work as waitresses, and close to 2 million work as bookkeepers. These women by and large do not experience the world of work as liberation from the drudgery of child rearing. For them, it is work that is drudgery and child rearing that is liberating.

Even women who work in jobs they once found exciting and stimulating often don't feel the same way after they give birth and are startled by how much they enjoy being mothers. They are forming something of a backlash movement against the executive "supermom" of the 1980s, who attempted to balance briefcase and baby, and instead are quitting their careers in order to do what we heard women would never do again—that is, move to the suburbs and raise kids. "Growing up in the slipstream of feminism, my friends and I had definite notions of what we would do when we grew up. We would become pilots, lawyers, actresses, photographers, and tycoons. Never, ever would any of us settle for being just a housewife," observes former radio correspondent Meghan Cox Gurdon in a 1997 essay. But, she goes on to say, with some embarrassment, "Reader, I *am* a housewife. I'm acquainted with scores more. And not one of these women . . . are bored, foolish, or frustrated. None of us is even overweight. Of the two dozen housewives I know best, all but one has at least a bachelor's degree. Most of us left successful, professional careers after our children were born, and most of us are in our thirties. At our coffee mornings—yes! we do sometimes meet for coffee!—we talk politics as much as we do infant feeding schedules. . . ." But it is still considered a socially awkward choice for a smart, ambitious woman to make. As Gurdon writes, "I ran into a former colleague recently, a radio correspondent who, like me, has lived around the world and reported dangerous and thrilling stories. Her face crinkled with incredulity when I told her of my current goings-on. 'But what do you *do?*' Ah. This is the great unanswerable question, the one dinner party query that leaves all but the most self-assured housewives gasping like beached tuna."

The question is only unanswerable, however, in a society in which the virtues of work have been so inflated that we can no longer appreciate anything that's not accompanied by a paycheck. When feminists elevated the status of work women did outside the home over what they did inside it, it was hard for mothers to answer back—as it is still hard for them to answer back. The joy mothers take in their children, the satisfaction they feel raising them into useful and decent citizens, are intangibles that cannot be neatly lumped into statistics; nor will their proceeds purchase a sports utility vehicle or some other trapping of worldly success. The rewards of a job are measurable in ways you can convey to other people, particularly those without children: I earn XX amount; I finished a lengthy report; my sales commissions went up XX percent last year. No one gets paid for being a mother—if anything, it's a colossal net loss, and the love you feel for your child, the love you receive back, is utterly untransferable. To onlookers he is just another drooling, runny-nosed, whining impediment to getting things done. It may be true that thirty years ago shockingly discriminatory attitudes toward women in the workplace prevailed, and we are all thankful to be rid of them. But in their place have risen some shockingly discriminatory attitudes toward women who wish to have children without neglecting them (as exemplified by Hillary Clinton's remark, "I suppose I could have stayed home and baked cookies"). And it is these attitudes that have made it difficult for a woman today to occupy either sphere of work or home completely happily, without feeling guilty and exhausted in one or insecure and underappreciated in the other.

The so-called progressive solutions advocated on behalf of working mothers merely aggravate this tension. Labor unions decry third world factories where workers stitch and assemble with children at their feet. But in the sleek setting of managerial America, this same practice is being hailed as a creative way to combine motherhood and work. Some companies are opening sick rooms for employees' children, staffed by nurses, so a parent never has to take a day off to care for a sniffling son or daughter. They can pull their children from their beds, haul them to work in the car, and deliver them into cots to be under the watch of "caring professionals." Cutting-edge day-care centers are installing cameras that parents can access on the Internet from the office. Other companies allow employees to bring their infants to the office, and are experimenting with ways to allow for breast-feeding on the job. In 1998, the visitor's bureau of Lake County, Indiana, issued a press release bragging that it would now permit newborn to six-month-old babies to accompany staff members into the office where they could sleep in cribs near their mothers and fathers. "The sound of a Winnie the Pooh music box mixes with the beeps and whistles of faxes and computers," boasted the release. The head of the bureau extolled the benefits of the new policy: "The time and resources saved by having the employee in the office greatly overcomes any loss of time due to limited distraction." Of course, the bureau didn't offer any observations on where it expects parents to put their children *after* those first six months.

No one seems to find any of these solutions creepy. But think, what these policies are saying to women is this: You must never, ever *think* about taking five minutes away from the office, not even for a newborn child. Is he sick? Bring him along and let our nurses care for him. Is he too little to be left alone in day care? Well, put a crib in your office and you can make those important calls while breast-feeding!

And what do these policies say, too, to the children? From their earliest memories, the love they receive and the attention they get will have been squeezed in around office schedules and ringing phones. Home will be for them the place of emotional upheaval and flashing tempers and food gulped in front of the television; it will be their day-care centers that offer them stability, security, and people who care that they have learned to stack blocks and mold Play-Doh. Yet "hunger for their mother isn't something babies can just 'get over,' " wrote editor Karl Zinsmeister in the May/June 1998 issue of *American Enterprise* magazine. "The question is not whether hired day care should exist (it always will), or whether it should be made as good as possible (of course it should). The question is whether everyday middle-class Americans should produce children without the intention of nurturing them. There is a difference between a compromise made in reaction to some crisis of fate and an arrangement made simply because one wants to maximize one's own position while ignoring serious costs to others."

We shouldn't need scientific research to tell us something so obvious; the people we should be listening to are not scientists at all but our own children. So far as I know, there has never been a poll done on three- and four-year-olds, but if there were, I doubt the majority would say that they are "happier" and "better off" with their mothers away all day. One day as I picked my son up from nursery school, a little girl in his class ran up to tell me, with breathless excitement and shining eyes, that her *mother* was coming to pick her up and they were going to spend the *whole* afternoon together and the *whole* evening, too, which they *never* got to do! I thought, Wow! What a rare treat! Time with Mom!

From a child's point of view, there can be no such thing as "quality care." A baby is unaware of the economic necessity that may cause his mother to be absent from him. A toddler cannot understand the personal satisfaction a mother experiences spending her day pursuing the brass ring instead of stacking plastic rings with her. A six-year-old is indifferent to the arguments of why it is important for women to be in the office rather than at home. What children understand is what they experience, vividly, every day, moment to moment; and for thousands of children who are placed into full-time care before they have learned to express their first smile, that is the inexplicable loss of the person whom they love most in the world. Twenty years ago, psychologists caught up in the intellectual fashions of the moment insisted that divorce was not only fine for children, it was *good* for them: Kids, they insisted, did better with one parent than with two who were unhappily married. Now that the children of that generation have grown up, the data are irrefutable: Divorce, however good it might be for parents, has been a disaster for children. I often have the sense, when I hear day-care advocates extol its benefits, that the result of their experiment will be equally catastrophic when the results are measured a decade or two from now. Then again, we may not have to wait quite that long for the answer.

The writer Anne Roiphe, in her 1996 book about motherhood, *Fruitful*, tells this story: "At an academically excellent all-girls private school on the Upper East Side of Manhattan a few years back, the principal held a special assembly so the girls could meet a woman who was a partner in a major law firm and had just been asked to serve on an important city commission. . . . The lawyer spoke to the girls about her work, her training, and her interest in First Amendment issues. When she finished, the first question asked was what hour did she get home. The second question was who took care of her children during the day. The third question was about what happened if one of her children was sick. The students, most of them daughters of working women, professional women who had left their children in the care of au pairs, nannies from Jamaica or Trinidad, did not take kindly to this lawyer and her accomplishments. They hissed her answers to those questions."

Sue Shellenbarger, the "Work & Family" columnist for *The Wall Street Journal*, encountered a similar attitude among a group of Nebraska teenagers of working parents she interviewed in 1998: "Despite widespread criticism of working parents, most of the teens give their parents' generation high grades," wrote Shellenbarger. "But many (including some with a parent at home) describe their family lives as nearly barren of relaxed time together and say they wish for more leisurely time spent talking with their parents as peers. Though they expect it to be difficult, most vow to spend more time with their children."

The relaxed time that the teenagers crave is the essence of family life, and something we lose when we are away from our children at work. Offices don't prepare us for being mothers: Children don't like playing games or having conversations on a schedule; they do not reserve all their important moments of growth for off hours and weekends. Authors like Susan Chira may insist that they are every bit as involved in their children's lives as mothers who work less or not at all because, as Chira once said, her children are in her heart and she is in theirs. But just being "in their hearts" is not enough (a friend of mine, upon hearing this, remarked that Chira was speaking of herself as if she were dead—"I live in their hearts . . ."). We must be there for them in body as well as in spirit. I've noticed that when you work, you try to make up for the time you're not with your children by being overly involved with them; but what they really prefer, particularly as they get older, is for you to be *there* but distracted. They can ask you things as the thoughts occur to them; color a picture without you checking your watch; play by themselves while you're nearby, busy with some chore; go for a walk in the park because the weather at that moment happens to be lovely; and see neighboring friends on the spur of the moment without elaborate play dates having to be arranged to suit everyone's timetable. It is these trivial, daily, and seemingly mundane moments that compose a childhood. And they are moments a mother never gets back. The length of time it takes for a human being to transform from a demanding infant into a smiling baby into a crawling terror into a walking child into a teenager and finally into a grown man or woman is profoundly short. Years later, a mother looks at baby photos and hungrily tries to recall the powder scent of her children's skin, the soft indents on the back of their necks, the pudginess of their feet, how she could cradle their entire bodies in her arms. Where did that all go, so quickly? As my mother-in-law once said, wistfully staring at a picture of her daughter when she was a baby, "You can't have them back like that ever again, not even for *one minute.*"

When you think about it, it seems a poor trade-off for a society: valuing the work a woman does writing legal briefs more than the hours she might have devoted to helping her child feel her importance in the world. It is sad that in the space of a generation motherhood has sunk from being regarded as a strong, noble, and vital task to one that garners pity at best, contempt at worst. Until we acknowledge that not only do children need their mothers but that mothers need their children, and that this is neither bad for women nor a sign of weakness, we will never be equal to men in the ways *we* care about—only, at best, equivalent in our statistical output and our monetary income. A prominent Canadian feminist once remarked to me that "artificial wombs could not be invented quickly enough" for her. I had to admire her remark for its stark, if ghoulish, candor. She understood that what keeps women from realizing perfect economic equality with men are those inconvenient threads that bind us to our children. From her point of view, we needed to snip those threads and raise babies from harvested eggs on farms, like fish.

It may be that equality for women, *true* equality for women, will rest in the acceptance that we *can* have it all—but that we cannot have it all at once. We needn't surrender our aspirations outside our families. But we will have to plan and arrange our lives better in order to realize them. The average American woman of my generation will live eighty years. She will probably work for forty of those years. But for six or seven or eight of those years she will be a mother to very young children. Does it make sense for society to reinvent itself so that she can more conveniently and inexpensively delegate the care of those babies to strangers? Or would it be better for society to try and figure out a way to help her care for them herself and then return to work when her children are in school (or not return, if that is her preference)?

It may seem radical to phrase the question this way, to assert that the solution to the work/family dilemma involves imagining ways to help mothers of young children stay home. But if it does seem radical, that only shows how deeply the feminist beliefs about the primacy of work over family, autonomy over motherhood, have been absorbed. I'd like to think that an enlightened society is not one in which all its economic and cultural forces combine to encourage women to deposit their children in state crèches and walk away without a backward glance. And if I'm right, then any solution *must* begin with the recognition that women need help getting time *away* from the workforce to be with their young children and *not*, as the current advocates would have it, in subsidizing day care to free Mom to go to work to pay the taxes to fund day care.

In the end, changing government policy can only do so much. Ultimately, the solution to The Problem will rely upon changing our own attitudes toward the value we place upon work. So long as we insist upon defining our identities only in terms of our work, so long as we try to blind ourselves to the needs of our children and harden our hearts against them, we will continue to feel torn, dissatisfied, and exhausted. Is this unfair? Maybe. But it is an issue to take up with nature, not politicians. We are the most radically equal generation of women in human history and we have collided with one of the oldest facts of our sex. There may be ways to ease our situation, but we cannot change it. Nor should we want it to be changed. The guilt we feel for neglecting our children is a by-product of our love for them. It keeps us from straying too far from them, for too long. Their cry *should* be more compelling than the call from the office.

chapter five

About Aging

THOSE WHO lead revolutions eventually get around to writing their memoirs and when they do, the first question they must ask themselves is, Was it worth it? The baby boom feminists are now entering their fifties, sixties, and seventies. They too are producing volumes of autobiography. In answer to the question, Was it worth it? their words assure us that it was. Yet everything about the way their lives turned out contradicts them.

If freedom from traditional roles and the pursuit of independence leads to female happiness, then those women who achieved these things should be living the most contented, fulfilled lives. And indeed, when you pick up the many memoirs by feminists that have been published over recent years, their tone is invariably upbeat. However turbulent life has been for them, the authors of these books insist, their feminist beliefs have never failed them, and they will even speak of their own aging as just another phase of "liberation" in the long process of realizing themselves as strong, unconventional, and fiercely free women. When you reach fifty or sixty or seventy, they tell us, you experience something like a rebirth: Children are grown and out of the way. You're no longer preoccupied with your appearance or weight or sex life. You might even leave a husband who has grown stale and familiar in order to achieve long-suppressed ambitions—attending law school, for example, or trekking through the Himalayas.

The late poet May Sarton told a surprised college audience, "I love being old." Being seventy, she said, was "the best time of my life" because "I am more myself than I have ever been. There is less conflict. I am happier, more balanced, and more powerful." Carolyn G. Heilbrun, in her 1997 book, *The Last Gift of Time: Life Beyond Sixty*, describes her relief at being able to wear comfortable clothing—jeans, sweats, and sneakers— wherever she pleases, without feeling the need to make excuses. At her fiftieth birthday party, Gloria Steinem told her friends that "Fifty is now what forty used to be. We can choose younger men." (Well, *some* of us can.) Writer Gail Sheehy insists in her 1995 book, *New Passages*, that we shouldn't in fact refer to ourselves as "aging" at all but as "saging"—"the process by which men and women accumulate wisdom and grow into the culture's sages." To celebrate their "new" older selves, these women will stage "coming out parties" or take cruises with female friends. Or they invent their own birthday "rituals," like the woman, who, according to *The Washington Post*, "made her friends line up and form a tunnel with their legs which she then slid through as a symbolic 'rebirthing canal.' "

Between the lines of these assurances that growing old is *just great*, however, you can't help but get the impression that these women's own lives have *not* actually turned out as they'd wished; that their politics have not protected them from the loneliness and physical betrayal of later life. Betty Friedan writes appreciatively, in her 1993 book, *The Fountain of Age*, of the circle of friends and relatives that sustains her into her seventies and about all the adventures she takes, like an Outward Bound course. But she admits, too, that she has obtained her contentment only by accepting that she will never enjoy the intimacy and companionship of a husband or lover again. "Intimacy with whom—if you're a woman alone, widowed, or divorced as more and more of us now are?" she wonders. "There came a time when I simply stopped having the old sexual fantasies. I no longer even dreamed of remarrying. I knew the odds, the numbers, only too well. I went on about my business—lectures, teaching, writing, conferences, children, grandchildren, friends, trips, dinners. And I didn't let myself feel the panic: Would I never know true intimacy again, would I ever take off all my clothes, be completely there with another being again? And sometimes I felt such a yearning, such a sense of loss, that I desperately tried playing the old game again. But it no longer worked. I couldn't do it. I couldn't risk the shame. Better to face the fact that this part of my life was over and take what pleasure I could in children and friends, women and men, without wanting or expecting it to end in bed, much less romance or marriage." A friend of hers offers an even harder assessment: " 'Be honest,' my friend Martha said. 'We all have the same problem and there's no solution for it. All these women, widowed, divorced. The men our age are married, if they're still alive. And if they get widowed or divorced, they go after younger women, who still want them, if they have money, any power at all. No one even looks at us that way anymore. Of course, we have our women friends, the children, grandchildren, if we're lucky. But it's not enough. It makes me mad just to think about it.' "

Then there are those women who are entering late middle age and menopause and feeling keenly the loss of their beauty. In a less progressive time, when women realized little more in their lives than their destinies as mothers and wives, this was the wrenching moment, according to Simone de Beauvoir, when a woman "loses erotic attractiveness and the fertility which, in the view of society and in her own, provide the justification of her existence and her opportunity for happiness. With no future, she still has about one half of her adult life to live." But today's women—and even today's feminists—feel the fading of their physical charms no less keenly. Germaine Greer, once considered the sexiest of the 1970s libbers, has spoken angrily about her sudden "invisibility" in the eyes of men after she reached a certain age. At thirty-seven, *Nation* columnist Katha Pollitt admitted that, "as a sex object, to put it bluntly, I am depreciating by the day." In her 1996 book, *Getting Over Getting Older,* feminist Letty Cottin Pogrebin describes her own physical decline: "I had the exact same body until I was forty-nine and suddenly everything started falling down. I woke up in the morning and suddenly my neck was gone. My chin had melted. You'd have to be completely oblivious not to notice. You'd have to be not living in your body not to notice."

These women's lives may be filled with interesting work, but as women they have only belatedly discovered that their personal lives cannot transcend the barriers that their professional lives could. If they are not watching younger women marching off with their male peers, they are realizing much too late the value of attachments they shunned in their more ambitious—and attractive—youth. In a *Washington Post* feature on baby boomers turning fifty, a single woman who decided to join the Peace Corps for an adventure tells the reporter, "In the last year and a half, I've come into a sense of myself and a sense of my worth." But she goes on to say that she "always assumed that [she] would marry, own a home, and raise a family, but none of that has happened so far." And then this heartbreaking anecdote: Twenty years ago, she says, when she was traveling in Italy, "I bought the sweetest little pair of baby booties—white with a little pink rose. They were for me and my baby." Not long ago, she gave them away.

Betty Friedan, in her 1983 essay, "Thoughts on Becoming a Grandmother," describes taking her new grandson to visit three childless female friends of hers, all single psychotherapists approaching their forties. She is bemused at how these "psychological amazons" begin "devour[ing] him with unscientific attention," babbling away at him and making faces. After she goes home, the women apparently stay up late into the night, discussing the pros and cons of having babies without husbands. Friedan observes, "In the last few months . . . at least six women in their mid-thirties and early forties have asked my advice about having a baby 'by myself.' They are women who spent their twenties and thirties concentrating on career, some of them after the disillusionment of too-early marriages, followed by divorce. Now, either they are involved with men who've had enough troubles with their own kids and want no more, or they are not in an intimate relationship with any man, and do not want or expect to marry again. A few have become lesbians. But, up against the biological clock now, they seem to feel an overpowering urge to have a baby. 'I give myself till I'm thirty-eight,' one says. 'Then, if I haven't found anyone, I'll go ahead anyhow and have a kid by myself. The question is, shall I use a sperm bank and artificial insemination, or shall I ask a friend?' "

That a father—in human form, not just biological—might be necessary and important to a child is a factor that does not enter into these women's equations. They have lived for themselves; they are used to living *by* themselves; and now they want the benefits of a baby without the messy entanglement of marriage. Some women push the envelope of reproductive technology and wait until fifty to bear babies alone—like the new mother interviewed by *The New York Times Magazine* for a story entitled "How Old Is Too Old?": "One day she realized she was nearly fifty. She was a corporate executive living with her elderly parents. She was healthy—exercising regularly, eating right. And with a job she loved and a family she was close to, she was relatively happy. But she wanted more. . . . 'When my son is twenty, I'll be seventy-one, [she said.] That doesn't sound too old to me.' "

But whether a woman has a baby for selfish reasons or not, married or not, waiting has its consequences for those less lucky with the high roll-of-the-dice odds the technology offers. "In the early 1970s," writes Anne Taylor Fleming, author of the 1994 book, *Motherhood Deferred*, "when my husband, Karl, whispered above me about wanting to have a baby, I shrank from his ardor. I couldn't imagine it, didn't even feel the connection between lovemaking and baby-making, so methodically had I put contraception—and ambition—between my womb and pregnancy." Years later, at age thirty-eight, she finds herself "driving down the Santa Monica freeway with a jar of my sixty-year-old husband's sperm in my purse, en route to the Institute for Reproductive Research at the Hospital for the Good Samaritan in downtown Los Angeles." She joins the other women in the waiting room of the clinic who "have sailed together into a strange, surreal country, the Country of the Disembodied Procreators, mutually dedicated to practicing biological warfare against our very own bodies in the hope of reversing time, cheating fate, and getting our hands on an embryo, a baby, a life." As she drives back down the highway, she is tempted to roll down her car window and shout: "Hey, hey, Gloria! Germaine! Kate! Tell us: How does it feel to have ended up without babies, children, flesh of your flesh?! Did you mean to thumb your noses at motherhood, or is that what we heard or intuited for our own needs? Simone, Simone de Beauvoir and Virginia Woolf, can you wade in here too, please, share any regrets, my barren heroines from the great beyond? Tell me: Was your art worth the empty womb . . . ? The clouds do not part; no feminist goddess peers down with a benediction on my emptiness. I am on my own here, an agnostic midlife feminist sending up silent prayers to the fertility gods on high. (I also send up apologies to the mothers of yore, the station-wagon moms with their post-partum pounds who felt denigrated in the liberationist heyday by the young, lean, ambitious women like me so intently making our own way.)"

If there was one sacred belief of feminism, it was that biology is not destiny. But reading these musings by older women, I'm reminded of the anthropologist Lionel Tiger's remark that if biology is not destiny, it is "good statistical probability." The life that is lived for oneself, or for one's external accomplishments, is no less superficial or doomed to defeat than that of the beauty queen who seeks to extend her power with face-lifts and exercise or of the housewife who seeks to live indefinitely through her children. Age eventually catches up and forces a person to reckon with what is important in life and what counts as achievement. As de Beauvoir wrote about the woman who invests everything in her femininity, at a certain age the moment comes "to draw a line across the page, to make up her accounts: she balances her books. And she is appalled at the narrow limitations life has imposed upon her." But life is no less narrow, as this generation of women has discovered, if you invest everything in attempting to escape the bonds of anatomy. You finally feel the readiness to become a mother at forty and are appalled to find out you can never become one. Or you divorce at fifty and are appalled to realize you may never share the intimate company of a man again. Or you deny your children your company while they are growing up in order to pursue a career, and are appalled by their indifference, even hostility, toward you when you seek their company as an old woman. And this is maybe the cruelest irony of the attempt to deny our biology's importance: It has only made it more critical and looming in our lives as we age.

◆ ◆ ◆

THIS WAS not how it was supposed to be. Feminists thought they could liberate themselves from the pressures of age and beauty if they liberated themselves from dependency upon men. By not shaving their legs and underarms, by refusing to wear makeup and high heels, they could poke the male aesthetic in the eye and announce to the world that they were unwilling to do anything to their appearance to please men, including bathe. Unfortunately for the women's movement, of all the laws it managed to abolish or reverse, it could not repeal the laws of sexual attraction. Men and women still go to great lengths to make themselves appealing to each other, and in very traditional ways. It is still true that most men, given a choice, will prefer a younger woman to an older one, a prettier one to a plainer one, a more curvaceous one to a less endowed one, one in a short skirt to one in pants—just as most women, given a choice, will prefer a tall man to a short one, a thick-haired one to a bald one, a manly one to a wimpy one, a successful one to an unsuccessful one. Women, no matter how rich or powerful they might be, will still be inclined to wince when they pass a mirror after forty, just as a man in his eighties will still have the impulse to snap his head around as a sexy woman passes by him on the street.

What has changed, though, is the status and protection a woman enjoys in her marriage after her sexual power has diminished. As divorce has become more accepted and easier to obtain, the pressure upon a wife to be an attractive, sexual creature in the eyes of her husband has increased, not decreased. De Beauvoir may write scathingly of the "parasitical" wives of her time, whose purpose in life, as she saw it, expired when their children left home. But what of that familiar figure of our time— the discarded graying first wife who is forced to start her life over again at fifty or sixty because she could not compete sexually with a woman twenty years her junior? Our grandmothers didn't feel any less than we do the loss of their beauty or their waning sexual power. But at least they could greet age with a certain amount of dignity, knowing the years they had spent upon their husbands and families in their youth entitled them to loyalty and respect in their old age. And they could count upon the security that came from the condemnation society poured upon men who abandoned wives after they'd ceased to be sexually useful.

Now every woman, unless she is very confident of her marriage or does not mind spending her later years alone, feels compelled to become the modern version of the sad, aging beauty queen, desperately trying to extend the life of her sexual power. According to the American Society of Plastic and Reconstructive Surgeons, the number of patients having face-lifts went up by 50 percent between 1992 and 1997. The same survey shows three times as many younger women (nineteen to thirty-four years old) having breast implant surgery. As Pollitt wrote bitterly, "Today I am urged on every side to fight the encroaching decay of my person with large investments of energy, time, and money. I should slather my face with makeup by day and collagen cream by night. I should take up aerobic dancing and resign myself to 1,200 calories a day for life. I should dye my hair. Advertising, which features no female who looks one minute over twenty-five, tells me this, and so do women's magazines, which treat beauty care and dieting as a female moral duty. . . . Does this mean I accept my age gracefully? No, actually I'm furious . . . and frightened—when I think of the time down the road when I'll be elderly in more than the obstetrical sense. Will I end up tied to a bed in some horrible nursing home?" Helen Bransford, in her 1997 book, *Welcome to Your Facelift*, acknowledged that she is the daughter of a Southern belle, "an arresting beauty with alabaster skin and 200-watt blue eyes," who, she said, would never have felt the need to have a face-lift. Bransford is similarly blessed with good looks, but she decided to undergo the operation at forty-seven: "I always knew there'd be a price to pay for marrying a man seven years younger than I am," she wrote, tacitly admitting that the mere fact that she is the mother of toddler twins with her husband, novelist Jay McInerney, does not give her enough confidence that he will stick around as she ages. After her operation, she said, "I had no idea that after a face-lift I would feel so liberated. I was feeling apologetic about having extra skin under my throat. . . . Our society is skewed so women have much greater pressure about their looks. If there's this single thing they can do to restore confidence, it's not that big a deal."

And perhaps it shouldn't be a big deal. But in a sneering review of Bransford's book, a feminist critic for *The Washington Post* taunted the author for her "unabashed embrace of superficiality" when she should have instead attempted to "[deliver] a left hook to the patriarchal monster." To which one can only say, Well, there's good advice. And where might we find this patriarchal monster to which to deliver the said left hook? But it is typical of feminists to deny or mock the fears of women like Bransford or to blame the "patriarchal monster" instead of acknowledging the obvious, if vexing, biological fact that women become less attractive to men as they age. More ardent feminists declare this attitude as "ageist": For men to view a sixty-year-old woman as less sexually appealing than a thirty-year-old is considered a form of discrimination. As in so many other areas of life, men must be retrained to appreciate the alluring qualities of crow's feet and liver spots: "If we can never feel that mysterious attraction bubbling up towards an old woman, a disabled woman, an Hispanic woman, we can pretty well suspect that we are oppressive to such women in other ways," says feminist writer Cynthia Rich in an essay entitled "Ageism and the Politics of Beauty." Therefore, "[we] can recognize that ideas of beauty are socialized into us and that yes, Virginia, we *can* begin to move in the direction of resocializing ourselves. We can work, for ourselves and for any revolution we might imagine, to develop a deeper and more resonant—dare I say more *mature*—concept of beauty."

Of course no woman should cease to be loved simply because she is old. But a society that refuses to acknowledge that age touches women very differently from the way it touches men—a society that shrugs as good enough marriages are dissolved after twenty or thirty years—is a society condemning millions of women to loneliness. And any ideology that justifies or excuses easy exit from marriage cannot honestly claim to defend the interests of women. Feminists who say that it is only prejudice that stops men from being physically attracted to old women or who tell women to fight the patriarchy when they worry about their looks will not help women feel less insecure. They'll take the face-lift, thanks. "Feminism has not made the woman past her prime into an object of envy," writes Anne Roiphe in *Fruitful*. "She is still considered sexless, unlike the male of the same age, no longer beautiful, her powers dying on the vine. If she has succeeded in work she may take comfort in her position in the world, but her womanliness is not at high tide, regardless of how the juices may run in her imagination. She is a biological creature with no further biological potential. Despite what the feminist movement says, this affects her power in the world. You can't dismiss anatomy with a wave of the wand. We are creatures designed for evolution's purpose. . . . It's not what feminists would wish but it is so."

DENYING THAT biology has any say over destiny also means denying that there are phases of a woman's life that are naturally suited to phases of her biology. A sixty-year-old woman shouldn't have to be thinking about dating or "starting over" unless she's widowed, and a fifty-year-old should not have to be chasing a toddler around a park unless it's her grandchild. But these are the incongruous lives so many older women now find themselves living.

When I was pregnant with my first child, in my late twenties, my obstetrician was a jovial man in his early fifties. His office shelves were cluttered with the successive school portraits of his children, culminating in their graduation pictures. Scattered between them were the lumpy, handmade gifts of a dozen Father's Days—clay tablets with I LOVE YOU DAD painted in squiggly letters, rock paperweights, and decoupage picture frames. During one of my monthly appointments, he told me how he'd been out to dinner the night before with some friends, a man his age who had divorced and remarried a much younger woman, now pregnant. "Can you believe it?" he asked me, with both horror and amusement. What was there to believe? I replied. It happened all the time. "No, no, just try to imagine it," he continued. "My last kid [he pointed to one of the pictures] just graduated and moved out. Hallelujah! My wife and I are now *free*. We're starting to plan trips for the first time *in years*. Can you imagine starting over again, at my age? Good God—changing diapers, waking up in the middle of the night . . . I mean, if my wife came home and told me, miracle of miracles, that she was pregnant again, I would give her the abortion *myself.*"

I didn't fully appreciate my doctor's point until after my baby was born. The phenomenon of starting families in later life wasn't confined to men leaving their wives for younger women. The first time I pushed my newborn daughter to the playground, I was struck by how many grand-mothers were sitting on the park benches and along the sides of the sand-box, tending to their grandchildren. After a few more outings, it dawned on me that these women weren't the children's grandmothers but their *mothers.* Some of them had gray-streaked hair; others, lined faces; all were wearily trying to keep up with the energy of their high-voltage two-year-olds.

The more I watched them, the more fascinated I became with what had become the accepted wisdom in circles of ambitious women—that it was better to postpone having children until after you had established your-self in your work. Even some baby experts assert the view that older women often make better mothers. Just as feminist writers like Carolyn Heilbrun insist old age is the best phase of her life because she is at last free to be herself, so is there a school of thought that justifies postponing motherhood into one's forties when one's identity is "set" and cannot be undermined by the arrival of a baby. In the words of family therapists like Carolyn Alton Seigal, "An older mother has a greater sense of herself. She's had the opportunity to work out issues of self-esteem and indepen-dence." Professor Caryl Rivers, who has studied women and families at Boston University, agrees: "Older mothers have a head start on not let-ting their children define them." And it is this elite attitude that no doubt has influenced the general statistical trend among women—particularly educated, white career women—to postpone having children. Between 1980 and 1990, the number of women giving birth after the age of thirty-five nearly doubled; the birth rate for mothers over forty rose by 50 per-cent during the same time. Among my friends, then, I was considered something of a novelty by having a baby at twenty-eight. With one or two exceptions, none of my friends were having kids, and many weren't yet married. After my daughter was born, I felt suddenly and unspeakably old compared to my childless friends—unable to join them anymore on a whim for dinner or a movie, exhausted all the time, my life dictated by the tedious and constricting schedules of feedings and naps, and—nightmare of nightmares!—able to absorb myself for hours reading about such compelling issues as pacifiers vs. thumb sucking and when, precisely, to start solids.

Yet that first day in the playground I was surrounded by women in their late thirties and forties and beyond who had been out in the world for twenty years, wearing fitted silk suits, devoting their brains to the problems of mergers and corporate law, and all the while forging their fiercely independent identities. How much worse for them the upheaval of a baby! At their age, their own mothers would probably have been on the verge of seeing their last child out the door and enjoying the peace of their vacated houses. Now here they were, yanked out of their plush offices and forced to surrender their Italian leather briefcases for diaper bags bulging with enough supplies to get them through a week-long emergency evacuation. So much has been said about that generation of women who squandered their youth on their children, but wasn't it actually worse to be doing this all in one's midlife? Watching these tired women trying to look surprised and delighted at their child's inane burblings, I realized that it makes no more sense for a woman to have her first baby at thirty-eight or forty than it does at eighteen. Actually, it makes less sense. For all postponement of childbirth does—like the postponement of everything else that is important outside of our work—is to shove the labors and tensions of youth into a period of our lives when we are less able to cope with them and should by rights be free of them.

My own mother, for example, married and had children when practically every other woman of her generation did—in her early twenties. The standard feminist conception of what she did was to throw her life away and stymie her career. But this wasn't so—not in my mother's case, and not in that of the many great women of her generation (Sandra Day O'Connor and Jeane Kirkpatrick—to name just a couple—were stay-at-home mothers during their children's early years). By having her children young, she was free again in her early thirties to pursue her work as a journalist largely unhampered (and unresented) by her children, who were by then in school full-time. Her first marriage, to my father, ended when she was thirty-four, a still desirable and attractive woman. She re-married two years later—this time successfully—and is now, in her early sixties, a youthful grandmother who takes bicycling trips around the world with my stepfather and tirelessly keeps up with her three grand-children.

As it was, by the time I had my first baby at twenty-eight, I'd already wished I'd done it sooner. You are not forced to notice how old you actu-ally are until you've had a baby, and even by twenty-eight I was already less easygoing about the whole event than I would have been, say, at twenty-three. I was more distracted by my work and cared more about my time being wasted. I had less physical stamina; I fretted more about damage to my furniture (by then I actually *had* furniture). When I re-membered the life a woman in her early twenties leads—her ability to stay up to all hours, eat poorly, sleep over on friends' floors—I thought how much better suited that person is to the schedules and demands of a baby.

And better suited, too, in other ways, especially from the child's point of view. A child fits more naturally into a younger mother and father's life. It hasn't been born into a marriage whose patterns and routines are already long set, nor have five or six years of infertility problems resulted in the mother greeting the new infant like a tiny messiah. It is less likely to grow up an only child, and an only child who must shoulder alone, much sooner than others, the burden of old parents. The child of a younger mother will also, if he's lucky, know his grandparents and know them as energetic people, not as remote figures in anecdotes, as declining bodies in a nursing home, as graves to visit.

There is a photograph of my mother taken when I was an infant and my brother was three. I'm wrapped in a blanket and propped in the crook of her arm; my brother clutches her hand. We are gathered, improbably enough, in front of a palm tree in Honolulu. My mother, who was then twenty-eight, looks like a movie starlet, tanned and shapely in a tropical dress, radiating youth. There are other similar pictures of us lounging on the decks of ocean liners and playing on foreign beaches. My parents had very little money, but they were determined to see the world and saved whatever extra they earned for travel. They carted us along with them like so much extra luggage. I remember my friends' parents this way, too. During school parent nights, the hallways would be flooded with young men and women—not a gray hair among them (although of course to a kid, anyone over thirty still seemed impossibly old). I've attended numerous parents' nights at innumerable schools with my own children and am always startled to be surrounded by parents ten and fifteen years older than me, sitting awkwardly atop those little nursery-size chairs. Beside them their children are like darting missiles, effusing perverse enthusiasms for bugs, dinosaurs, and bathroom jokes, while they look on with detached bemusement.

This is the other side of aging, one the books that describe turning seventy as a great liberation don't like to dwell upon: We don't just physically age; we age psychologically as well. An older mother, aside from all the physical upheaval she will endure with a new baby, faces the problem of distance from her own childhood. She may, as experts insist, be more mentally prepared for motherhood than a younger woman. But she will certainly be further away from having natural empathy with her child, from that vivid sense of what it is like to be young. A woman who teaches postnatal classes to older mothers at Stanford University told me, "These are women who are accustomed to having control over their lives, and they try to control the babies' behavior and time. They overintellectualize the experience and are always looking to experts."

I've come across many mothers like this at my playground. One woman, who looked to be in her mid-forties, said that she hadn't gone out in the evening since her baby was born—in fifteen months!—because she didn't trust a sitter to put her child to bed. Another mother, in her late thirties, had a nine-month-old baby who was still waking up several times a night because the mother had decided that it would be traumatizing to let the child cry itself back to sleep. Other mothers were letting

their children stay up until ten and eleven every evening, reluctant to enforce bedtime out of fear it would cause personality disorders. I remember one serious-minded woman who asked me if I'd signed up my then
three-month-old daughter for swim classes at the Y. At first I thought
that these mothers had demanding careers and that their indulgence of
their babies arose from their daily distance from them. But no. As it
turned out, most of the older women with whom I struck up conversations had given up their lucrative jobs to be with their children. They'd
thrown themselves entirely into the task, as they had done when they
were lawyers or investment bankers. They worked at motherhood the
way they once would have worked on their most important accounts.
And when they'd stop their babies from stuffing sand in their mouths or
bonking another kid on the head, they'd speak to them as they would to a
subordinate at work who needed only a respectful, rational reminder not
to do it again.

These mothers were a stark contrast to the few younger mothers who
came to the park, and even the young nannies, who were often less con-
scientious but gave their children breathing space. They had not waited
half their lives to have these children. They did not want to live through
them (they just got out of childhood themselves, after all). And they were
still in that stage of life when they were blissfully unaware of their own
mortality: They did not cling to their children, savoring every precious
moment and fearing ever more intensely the day when their daughters or
sons took their first steps away from them.

It may not be so ironic, then, that the happiest memoirs among the elders of the women's movement are by those who led the most conven-
tionally female lives. They are the feminists who, despite all their
resentments and chafing at family life, managed to keep it and savor its
rewards in later life. Anne Roiphe devotes much of her book *Fruitful* to
the often guilty satisfaction she took in being a mother while her feminist

friends were off realizing themselves at marches or in therapists' offices: "I think that without my children, whatever I might be, I would be less, diminished, reduced, imprisoned inside my own skin, a person who will not leave a forward trace, the trail would only wind back." Heilbrun's memoirs rattle with the domestic clutter of dogs, houses, children, grandchildren, and the long, comfortable marriage to her (stoically patient) husband, whose bothersome habits, she concedes, "one now accepts, like a cat clawing the furniture." Betty Friedan takes enormous pleasure in watching her own children become parents and in being a grandmother. "I want this little Rafi to know me," she writes of her grandson. "I want to know this little person who is carrying my blood and energy and spirit into new life. His being gladdens my heart. I can't wait for him to start talking to me." Meanwhile, Gloria Steinem, alone in her fifties, devotes herself to writing a book about finding self-esteem.

What none of these women will do, though, is disavow any of the ideas that have left quite a few of their friends in less fortunate positions. The always observant Friedan notices some of the female wreckage around her, like the women who are chattering nervously about sperm banks, but she does not go much further than merely writing it down. Her daughter-in-law stops working after she has a baby, to Friedan's surprise and—to our surprise—approval. It's okay to stop working, Friedan assures us, if it's a "choice": "Given the strong feminist images of the family she married into, the fact that [my daughter-in-law] felt no need to apologize for having taken a 'hiatus' from any career bespeaks a real sureness of herself as a woman, which I applaud." Then she adds hastily, the blinkers going back on, "Don't get me wrong. I haven't gone back to the feminine mystique. I don't think having a baby is absolutely necessary, or even sufficient, for any and every woman's fulfillment." Anne Roiphe, despite her fine documentation of the bond between mother and child, and the enormous satisfaction that family life has brought her over the years, in the end advocates day care for children and demands, Soviet-fashion, for society to "change the emphasis from my child to our child, make the community care." These ladies keep chanting the word *choice* over and over, as if it meant anything at all. In their view, long-term traditional marriages, like motherhood, are okay if they're a "choice," just as lesbianism, single motherhood, and solitude in old age are okay so long as they're a "choice." The emptiness of this solution is apparent maybe only to those whose decisions left them without "choice"—those who did not "choose" to have their marriages end in their fifties, who did not "choose" to be infertile, who did not "choose" to discover that postponing everything of value in life could often leave them in a position when it was too late to achieve it at all, or leave one too old to enjoy it when it came. To these women, feminism offers no hope.

In that sense, female "liberation" has only ever been a viable idea to the young and unencumbered. It is only a young woman who can think about postponing life's big decisions to some dimly distant and unimaginable future. It is only a young woman who feels no sense of time weighing upon her, whose eyes have not yet begun to crinkle, who still feels sexually omnipotent. Feminism has never had anything useful or good to say about the ultimate consequences of liberation. When faced with women who postponed motherhood beyond their own ability to conceive, it can offer no consolation. When faced with women whose beauty and sexual power are draining from them, it can only say, Blame the patriarchy. When faced with women who are divorced and alone in old age, it tells them to learn to like being by themselves or to get a pet or to take up masturbation or lesbianism. (The last one is serious. Betty Friedan, in *The Fountain of Age*, quotes feminist therapists who bemoan the fact that more elderly women don't turn for love to themselves or to other women for their spinsterish comforts. Friedan cites a paper by Joy Spaulding, delivered to the Gerontological Society in San Francisco in 1983: "The older woman, faced with a distinct shortage of available men her age, might expand the options that she defines as acceptable to include masturbation, a relationship with another woman. . . . Some women choose a relationship with another woman as the preferred lifestyle and do not define it as an alternative to or substitute for a heterosexual relationship." And if these women don't want lesbian relationships? Friedan quotes a young student of gerontology at the University of Southern California as dismissing such an attitude as "old-fashioned." In a study the student did of elder people's opinions toward such sexual "options" as homosexuality and masturbation, she concluded, "This present-day cohort of older people grew up with a more close-minded attitude toward sex . . . that may prevent them from acting upon the suggestions for intimate relationships. . . .")

Dire, too, is an elder woman's financial situation if she has divorced. Her assets will have been divided; for many years after she has retired, she will have to eke out whatever remains of them, or rely upon the generosity of her children—if she's had any. She may take pride in the fact that throughout her life she hasn't depended upon men, but in her old age she may have to depend upon the state. Alas, she may then discover that the state is less reliable than a husband. As the baby boom generation ages, this may be the darkest surprise lurking for them ahead—how little the Social Security system will be able to offer them compared to their parents' generation. Yet how can they complain? The generation that placed their infants in day care should not be astonished when these infants grow up and take a dim view of their elders' demand to be supported by *them*.

Old age is, ultimately, reward or punishment for the lives we've lived. It's true that there will be women who find fulfillment in their solitary last years; who, like May Sarton, take enjoyment in their views of the sea, their vases of wildflowers, the company of their cats. But these lonely destinies are not the ones, I suspect, that most of us desire for ourselves. No matter how much success we may achieve in life, it is our families who sustain us; and how they sustain us depends very much upon what we've given them in return. In the end, it is our husbands and children and our grandchildren who we hope will be at our bedsides as the last light fades, holding our cooling hands.

chapter six

About the Political—and the Personal

THE LAST presidential election of the twentieth century was, in one sense at least, a triumph for women: In only seventy-seven years, we'd gone from being disenfranchised citizens to political love objects. Thanks to the widening "gender gap" (the phenomenon of women leaning to the Democrats while men preferred the Republicans), winning the female vote mattered more than it had in any previous election in American history. The ensuing 1996 campaign resembled not so much a run for high office as it did a contest between two suitors competing for the same woman's hand in marriage. Our wishes, our daily cares, and our changes in mood were measured by pollsters and worked into stump speeches by wily political consultants, who played Cyrano to the dumbstruck presidential candidates. By the final months of the campaign, not a day passed without some new flicker of light being shed on Freud's unanswerable question, "What does woman want?" One day it might have been a cleaner environment, the next safer streets, and the day after that school uniforms for our children and V-chips for our televisions. Reporters at *Newsweek* tracked down an individual they declared to be representative of the women's vote—a thirty-five-year-old single mother in Shrewsbury, Missouri—and followed her around for a day, noting everything about her, from her views on taxes to the cereal she poured for her son's breakfast.

This woman, they concluded, "is not in control of her life, but she is in control of this election."

Yet as we enter the next century, our first as fully enfranchised citizens, we should let that journalist's description of the typical female voter sit in our heads for a moment: *not in control of her life, but in control of this election.* The suffragists had once predicted that when women got the vote they would elevate political discussion. We would, in the words of Susan B. Anthony, "teach men a higher and nobler life than the one they now follow." Perhaps that may yet happen. In 1996, however, in our most influential election ever, the two major parties decided they must speak to us not as higher or nobler creatures than men but as more irrational, more emotional, and more self-absorbed.

We heard that women were put off by blunt language: "Women have a much lower tolerance for conflict," observed Democratic pollster Celinda Lake. "Take the [free] trade issue: Both parties kept making arguments for NAFTA by saying, 'This will increase competition.' But women don't like competition and they don't respond to metaphors such as 'leveling the playing field.' " We heard that women could not distinguish between their personal problems and the greater problems of society. When you spoke to women about crime, for instance, noted Republican pollster Kellyanne Fitzpatrick, women expressed more concern over the lighting of their streets or the safety of their parking lots than they did about broader issues, such as prison sentences or the death penalty. We heard that women even had trouble grasping big issues unless they were put to them in the simplest and most immediate terms. Tony Fabrizio, Dole's pollster, told *Newsweek*, "A male voter says, 'I'm getting taxed to death. I'm not making enough.' It's very cut and dried. With female voters, we hear, 'I'm working harder, but we're not getting ahead, and I don't have time to do everything I need to do.' Politics is much more contextual to a female voter than a male voter." "It's women who will be trying to figure out how to take care of Mom in old age," agreed Ann Lewis, the president's campaign manager. "To them this is not a technical issue. It's personal and it's visceral." And we heard that a candidate's position on the issues—whether it was reforming welfare or his stance on Social Security—was less important to women than whether he could emotionally "connect" with voters.

This became an especially dire problem for Republican candidate Bob Dole, who could no more emote than he could fly. Before the Republican convention in San Diego, Dole's strategist on women's issues, Linda Di-Vall, told *The New York Times*, rather wistfully, that she hoped her candidate would do "more personalizing" from the podium—perhaps by discussing his relationship with his wife or his upbringing in Kansas or his suffering from his war wounds. Unfortunately for his handlers, Dole could not be liberated from his self-restraint. When pushed, he would speak of things that were personal to him only in the most grimly taciturn way. This was not without a certain prewar charm, but his campaign team feared that women voters would not believe he was compassionate unless he could demonstrate personal weakness; would not trust him to govern unless he could claim to have experienced virtually every problem and pain a voter might complain of; would not remember his bravery in war unless he reminded them of it again and again.

Perhaps the most dismaying estimate of women, however, was that displayed at the party conventions. Ordinarily the business of conventions is for delegates to vote on the platform and to nominate a party's ticket. Critics grumble that in recent elections the actual business has been displaced by the opportunity to stage a three-day television commercial. In 1996, in the attempt to reach out to female voters, the events came less to resemble commercials than daytime programming on the Lifetime channel. At the Republican convention in San Diego, woman after woman ascended a lavender-lit podium to tell some heart-rending story about herself. A victim of AIDS spoke movingly about her suffering; she was followed by a victim of rape, who tearfully described her horrendous ordeal. Neither of these women made it clear what her story had to do with the November election. They—like the keynote speaker, Congresswoman Susan Molinari, who brought her baby with her to the convention hall—had been booked apparently solely for the emotional spectacle they would provide. The unspeakable crime that had been committed against the rape victim, the suffering of the AIDS patient, the baby who sucked a bottle on Daddy's lap while Mommy gave a speech—this was all now to be used to show women voters that Republicans *cared,* that they were in touch with their feminine side. As for the feminine side of the Republican candidate, that was left up to his wife, Elizabeth, to demonstrate. And she did, in an unprecedented speech in which she strolled through the audience with a hand mike, effusing about her husband's private qualities and tapping the shoulders of people he'd been good to in the past so they'd stand and smile for the camera. It would be hard to imagine an Eleanor Roosevelt or Abigail Adams making similar pitches—in essence, asking the public to vote for their men not because of the policies and principles they championed but entirely for the personal qualities that made them good husbands and friends.

Not to be outdone, the Democratic convention, held twelve days later in Chicago, offered up its own parade of victims—from the paralyzed actor Christopher Reeve discussing what it felt like to be handicapped, to the vice-president of the country describing his sister's death from cancer. The film that introduced President Clinton went nowhere near his policies or political achievements but instead dwelt at length upon the man's feelings about what it's like to be president and the incredible growing experience that the job had been for him.

Whether all this wooing actually had any effect on the female electorate is nearly impossible to tell. It didn't seem to help the Republicans, who were unable to improve their standing among women during the course of the campaign: Exit polls pointed to a seventeen-point overall gap between the sexes, which was consistent with the polls in the months leading up to the election. But the effect of the 1996 election on American politics is not so mysterious. Both parties have now come to an even more radical conclusion about women than the most militant feminists. They have decided that for women not only is the personal political but that *only* the personal is political.

This is the view, funnily enough, that antisuffragists put forth a century ago to justify denying women the vote. Women, they feared, would be unable to transcend their domestic concerns. They would drag politics into areas of private life where it didn't belong and look to government to solve the kinds of social and moral problems that were properly the responsibilities of family and church. "An essential weakness in the suffrage movement," wrote the nineteenth-century antisuffragist Elizabeth Jackson, "is the failure to distinguish between government and culture." We will witness the triumph of feeling over reason, the antisuffragists warned. Supporters of suffrage rightly insisted that these fears were based upon a demeaning view of women.

Yet in 1996 this demeaning view pervaded every campaign speech and commercial directed at us. No one—not in the press, not even in the biggest women's organizations of the nation—appeared insulted by it. Indeed, political discussion throughout the campaign kept returning to whether a candidate was exhibiting enough of this kind of behavior to appeal to women.

How did *this* happen?

FOR MOST of this century, there was no significant gap in the voting patterns between men and women, largely because, as author Steven Stark noted in the July 1996 issue of *Atlantic Monthly*, "men and women tended to define their interests mutually, in terms of their families, and to vote much the same." The differences that political analysts could actually discern on certain issues generally showed women to be slightly more conservative than men. Women tended to be more risk-averse— more likely to oppose war and the use of force and more inclined to favor incumbent candidates over challengers. Women, too, have historically been the greater champions of social issues, as in the crusades against prostitution and alcohol (it's not a coincidence that the women's suffrage and prohibition amendments to the Constitution were adopted within a year of each other) and in their support for the founding of the federal welfare state in the 1930s. As Stark observed, "New Deal social programs, such as the Social Security Act of 1935 and the Fair Labor Standards Act of 1938, were in part drafted and promoted by the old Progressive child-welfare establishment, dominated by women whose view of government reflected their maternal view of the state."

While there have been signs of women breaking away from male voters in the past—particularly during the 1970s in the fights over abortion and for the Equal Rights Amendment—the "gender gap" didn't become notable until 1980, with the election of Ronald Reagan. (According to exit polls, there was an eight-percentage-point gap between men and women: Reagan still beat Carter among women voters, but by a much smaller margin than among men.) As the gap persisted, strategists began to take an interest in the diverging voting patterns of the sexes, ones that culminated in the great gush of 1996. "Women," announced *The New York Times Magazine* in July of that year, "were [now] going off on their own, requiring special treatment."

As it turned out, however, it was only *some* women who were going off and requiring special treatment. The gap was not, as it has been starkly painted, simply a matter of women as a group voting differently from men; rather, it was *certain categories* of women voting differently from men. The so-called gender gap is actually a "marriage gap." While exit polls pointed to a seventeen-point overall gap between the sexes in 1996 among married women, the difference was quite small, only five points: 48 percent for the president vs. 43 percent for Dole. On the other hand, the president managed to charm fully 62 percent of single women.

This marriage gap, furthermore, was uniquely female. Men's political affiliations are not so easily discerned by their personal status. Just knowing a few facts about a woman's private life, however, enables a pollster to predict her stance on a whole range of political issues. While working on the Reagan reelection campaign in 1984, for example, Republican pollster Richard B. Wirthlin—the man credited with first noticing the gender gap in the polling data—broke women into thirty-two different categories, to which he gave names. "Some of these groups were more strongly Republican than males, others were ninety to ten against the Republicans," he told *The New York Times*. Reagan did best among the women Wirthlin called "Alice" (younger, married, working) and worst among "Helen" (younger, unmarried, not working). This "marriage gap" persisted in subsequent elections: In 1990, never-married women increased the gender gap when they voted, while currently married women reduced it, according to a study of historical voting patterns by economists John R. Lott, Jr., of the University of Chicago and Larry Kenny of the University of Florida.

In other words, the political change we have seen taking place over the past twenty years among women has less to do with their political differences from men than it does with their personal relations with them. Married women are voting the way they have always voted: They see their own interests intertwined with those of their husbands and children, and support the candidate they feel will best protect these interests. (In 1995, campaign adviser Dick Morris' polls showed Bill Clinton doing badly among married women with children. Morris insisted that the president take a well-publicized camping trip with his wife and daughter in order to make him more appealing to this group; alas for the president, who apparently hates camping, there was no subsequent "bounce" in the polls.) But, as Wirthlin perceived, many women now have much more tenuous and insecure intimate relationships. They may be single mothers on welfare, working mothers receiving day-care subsidies, divorced women without alimony, widows or single elderly women dependent upon Social Security and Medicaid. But they are women who look not to marriage for their economic security but to government—either in the form of direct subsidies and benefits or as an insurance policy against the day when the fathers of their children walk out on them. The study by Lott and Kenny concludes that there is evidence that "the gender gap in part arises from women's fear they are being left to raise children on their own. If this result is true, the continued breakdown of family and higher divorce rates implies growing political conflicts between the sexes."

Despite the celebration of women's gains in the workforce, women haven't become any less dependent as a result of the women's movement. They have just become dependent on different things. As divorce and out-of-wedlock births have skyrocketed over the past generation, the state has come to serve the financial function for women that men once did. Even the many millions of women who don't receive government handouts must now depend upon networks of loose and often impersonal ties that attempt to substitute for the once secure and singular relationship they would have had with a husband. These are women to whom a promise from government—even a vague assurance of, "Don't worry, we'll be here for you when things don't work out"—is the only promise of future security that they have.

The mother from Shrewsbury, for example, is unable to trust her future to the man she lives with—he has not, after all, made the commitment to marry her. Feminists may celebrate the "independence" of this woman, but she is hardly independent. She is dependent upon the goodwill of her boss and the market for used cars. She used to be dependent upon day-care workers to look after her son; now she must depend upon the health and patience of an aging mother. If any one of these people should fail her—if her boss lays her off, her boyfriend leaves, or her mother falls sick—her life falls in upon itself like a house of cards. Her entire story, as she tells it, is one of trying to keep everything together from day to day, with no certainty of being able to do so. And in this way her story *is* typical of thousands upon thousands of women across the country.

This pervasive feeling of female insecurity accounts, I think, for the peculiar emotional rhetoric that animated the 1996 election. As the Shrewsbury mother told *Newsweek*, she feels alienated from politics; it all seems "remote" and "useless." Why? As the reporters explained, "she has miniaturized . . . politics into a kitchen-table bargaining session over what it might take to help her get through the day." And from that point of view, the government has done little. "She has to pause and think a long time to imagine anything government has *done for her,* any difference it has made in her life, anything politics or politicians could ever *do for her* [emphasis mine]. 'Maybe I'll be able to get an SBA loan someday, start my own business.' " Thus, the defense and management of the freest, richest, most powerful and democratic country in the world does not count for very much in this woman's opinion of what politics actually does for her *personally.* Unless it lends her money—and maybe also comes home at night, takes out the garbage, oversees her son's home-work, and promises to love her forever—it's going to be a disappoint-ment.

The strategists in the 1996 election understood this. Female voters, they recognized, wanted order and authority from their government, but also emotional support and sympathy for their personal problems. Women wanted, in short, their politicians to be the fathers and husbands they didn't have in their own lives. "V-chips, computers in classrooms, school uniforms," said Don Baer, communications director of the White House. "They are all about giving [women] control of the lives of [their] children." Dick Morris recalls that during the campaign, "I drew on con-versations with [feminist author] Naomi Wolf, who had talked to me about the country's hunger for a good-father role model . . ." When it came time to put this idea into practice, he says, "I told the president, '[I]t's time to be almost the nation's father, to speak as the father of the country, not as a peer and certainly not as its child.' I urged him to stress family issues: the enforcement of child-support payments, the establish-ment of violence ratings for TV, improvements in education. These fit the image of a father concerned about America's children in a time when two-career families were stretched to the breaking point, growing fearful that their children were beyond their control. . . . I criticized the way he han-dled himself in public: 'You explain yourself too much. Fathers don't. You seem to care too much about what others think of you; that's not a fa-ther's way. Don't have conversations with your audience: speak *to* them . . ." He adds, "[Wolf] often said the candidate who understood the fatigue of the American woman would win."

That it may not be a politician's job to understand our "fatigue" or no-tice our headaches did not seem to have raised the eyebrows of the presi-dent's chief strategist. But that just goes to show how accustomed we are to turning to government to address the intimate problems of women's lives. If women are, understandably, "fatigued"—trying to raise their children, work at their jobs, carry their rents and mortgages, pay their bills and taxes, and plan for their retirement entirely single-handedly, all because they can't rely upon their lovers or husbands to hold up their end of the bargain—then it's natural they should turn to the increasingly paternal government to help them.

The issues Don Baer cited, for instance, are hardly those that should normally absorb a president. The V-chip, which would allow people to screen out television programs they don't want coming into their homes, may indeed appeal to huge numbers of working parents—and maybe, more specifically, to single working mothers who aren't around to discipline the TV-watching habits of their children. But the president, short of knocking on everyone's door at four in the afternoon and demanding that those eight-year-olds turn off MTV, can't discipline their children's TV-watching habits, either. Nor, for that matter, can the V-chip. It's just a piece of technology that some homes might have in the future while others won't (Sally will still watch MTV at Johnny's house). The same is true for computers in the classroom and school uniforms—both local school board issues. Yet as Dick Morris understood, just having the president talk about and "support" these things—never mind that they were beyond federal jurisdiction or beyond the scope of politics entirely—conveyed the kind of fatherly authority that is now absent from so many homes: Turn that junk off TV; don't fall behind in your studies; I'm not letting you leave the house looking like *that*.

In other issues the federal government attempted to redress our failed relationships. The president launched a strenuous campaign against "deadbeat dads"—those men who do not meet their child support payments and who, in many cases, leave their states to avoid prosecution—and advocated setting up a federal database to track down deadbeat dads. It was a politically safe issue as well: Who, after all, would side with deadbeat dads? And wasn't it understandable that women burned by a deadbeat dad would seek solace and help from their nondeadbeat government? Look at all that their government was promising or had done for them: a national system of government day care; the Family and Medical Leave Act.

Still, if the state might seem to be more dependable than many men, as a substitute for a husband's commitment, it's rather sinister. It's true that the state won't come home late at night stinking of drink. It doesn't shout at you or hit you or threaten to leave you when you've put on weight or a sexier woman comes along. And it's always there for you, in its big, lumpy, bureaucratic way. On the other hand, it's not very satisfying to lie next to or talk to, to grow old with or to love in return. And it can't love you, either, or be any sort of father to your children. And, perhaps not altogether surprisingly, the more pervasive the state grows, the scarcer decent, reliable men seem to become. As Virginia Woolf wrote in her 1938 political essay "Three Guineas," once women had the right to earn their own living and then, in her view, feminism became obsolete, what would we see? "Men and women working together for the same cause." Instead, as the 1996 election reminds us, men and women have seldom been more at odds with each other, nor have women ever been more divided among themselves.

THUS, THE DEBATE over women today has very little to do anymore with equality with men. By all objective measures, we have achieved and surpassed the goals that our suffragist ancestors could have imagined. I sometimes wonder what Lucretia Mott or Virginia Woolf would say if they could be transported through time and dropped on a street corner in New York or Washington. Would they be pleased—or shocked? They might shudder from the blast of a passing bus with a half-naked model plastered on its side or be startled by the sight of so many women wandering around wearing jeans, T-shirts, and nose rings. But as their modern-day Virgil took them both by the arm and began to explain all the things that American women could now do at the end of the twentieth century, they would certainly be staggered. Their guide would rattle off the statistics: Women may now work in any profession and expect to be paid the same as men. Women now account for more than half the degrees being awarded by universities. They may marry or not marry, divorce or not divorce, have sex or abstain, bear children or not, postpone or abort them—all without any social stigma. Look around you! the guide would tell these ancient ladies. Women are everywhere! In the office buildings, in the executive suites, in the state houses and the Capitol!

"And where are the children?" Miss Mott may ask. "Where do these women put all their children?" And here our guide might stammer a little as he thinks of a reply. "And who does the shopping and cleans their houses?" Mrs. Woolf might add, always practical. "Do the husbands help?" Miss Mott asks hopefully. "Sure they do," says the guide, muttering something about day care, the need for more of it, and of a few things not being worked out smoothly yet. "But they don't need husbands anymore!" he might say brightly. Their eyes widen. "They don't have to depend on them anymore, I mean—you know for money, that sort of thing." They nod politely, and continue touring. And what they discover, the more that they see, is that women have indeed achieved a rough parity with men—but at the expense of many other things that used to give them a sense of security, comfort, and purpose.

Women today may be leading more varied lives than they ever were, but our fundamental interests are unchanged. Those interests are rooted in the roles the vast majority of us eventually assume as wives and mothers, whether we continue to work or not. These are interests our society once recognized and sought to protect through our legal and social institutions. The women's movement attempted to replace women's natural alliance with each other—one that was based upon the defense of marriage and the family by law and custom—with a new "sisterhood" based upon women as a political class in opposition to men. To a great extent, the feminists succeeded. Women are more independent of men than ever. But for that independence, we have paid a heavy price. We receive more respect at the office but less respect as mothers. We lead more emancipated sex lives, but we have sacrificed male deference and commitment. We have more control over our professional lives, but we enjoy much less satisfaction in our personal lives. *Her life is a mess, but she's in control of this election.*

Women remain divided over whether our lives should take place mostly inside the home or mostly outside of it. We remain divided over whether we should put ourselves or our children and families first. We remain divided over who is chiefly responsible for providing for us and our children—our husbands and the fathers of our children or the state. And as a result, we are divided over political issues that are seen as benefiting one side at the expense of the other—the family vs. the individual woman.

Women like to pretend they are nonjudgmental creatures—we are masters of the tight smile—but we are all aware of the tension that crackles between working mothers and stay-at-home mothers, and between mothers and women who aren't yet. At school meetings and dinner parties, we may manage to pass an entire evening without dropping something like, "It must be boring for you all day at home," or, "Do your children miss you while you're at work?" or, "How nice for you not to be tied down by a baby." But the moral disapproval that each of these little remarks represents is something we've all felt radiating from women who've chosen to do things differently from us. And contained in the barb, too, is an acknowledgment of how these different choices threaten our own. The mother who works for personal fulfillment justifies leaving her children in the care of other people—whether they're relatives or baby-sitters or day-care workers—by convincing herself that if she stayed at home, she'd be bored and thus the children would be bored, too, or that it makes no difference to them whether she is there most of the time or not. How much happier they'd be in a stimulating environment, with a happy, fulfilled mother coming home every evening! A happy, contented, and intelligent housewife belies this woman's vision of the woman at home, and is irksome to the guilt and worry she feels about leaving her own kids. The happy, contented, and intelligent housewife, on the other hand, is threatened by the career woman whose status in society is superior to her own and who contributes to her household's expenses in a way the housewife's husband might envy. The married woman (and, more specifically, the married mother) is threatened by a single woman (and, more specifically, by an attractive single woman) because she is an irritating reminder of the sexual freedom that she and her husband have given up for domesticity. She might also be viewed as a threat to the stability of the married woman's marriage: No woman wants a hungry shark trawling near her shore. It is for this reason that women tend to seek similarity in their female friendships: Mothers at home socialize with other mothers at home, working women with other working women, and so on. It's not just about mutual interests but about mutual safety.

These tensions, which get suppressed in our private lives because they are too fraught to speak about honestly without causing pain or offense, erupt in our politics. If a woman feels that mothers ought to be spending more time at home, she will probably favor a tax cut or child deduction over higher government spending on day care. A female lawyer, however, might resent any insinuation from the tax department that nonworking mothers are entitled to benefits that she isn't, and lobby instead for a child-care deduction. Or, to use Helen and Alice from Wirthlin's poll, let's say Helen is the single mother of a two-year-old boy. The father of her child didn't stick around, or maybe he comes and goes, but either way, he doesn't help to support Helen and her son, so she's on welfare. Alice, let's say, is married and working in an office, perhaps as a data processor or assistant. She may have a child or is planning one. Alice resents her wages being taxed to help Helen, who, she thinks, shouldn't have had a child and ought to get a job. Or maybe she's a little more sympathetic to Helen but wants to have a family herself and doesn't see how she can afford to quit her job because her taxes are too high and her husband doesn't earn enough. And why are her taxes too high? Because, she might tell herself, there are so many Helens now dependent upon government; in her view, Alice is working to support Helen to stay at home, an option she'd like for herself. When it comes to politics, then, Alice likely wouldn't endorse subsidized child care or increased welfare benefits, but she would like a tax cut or child deduction that might allow her to quit her job or go part-time. She leans Republican, while Helen votes Democrat. In other words, the *differences* between these women are primarily moral, not political: They arise from diverging understandings of a woman's duties to her family and clashing beliefs about whom she should look to for support.

These moral differences explain the divide between women and the feminist politics of our day. Although feminist leaders are constantly warning that unless their policies prevail we'll all return to the rule of men, they are conjuring up a threat that doesn't scare anyone anymore, if it ever did. Lucretia Mott and Virginia Woolf, on their trip through time, would be hard-pressed to find any woman who didn't espouse what they would consider gratifying views about female emancipation, even among the so-called religious right. If they were to stop women on the street— the passing girl with the multicolored hair, the mother pushing the stroller, the bustling woman with the briefcase, the female college student hauling a knapsack stuffed with papers, the woman handing out JESUS SAVES flyers—and ask them their views on female equality, I doubt they would meet any woman who does not believe in equal opportunities for women, or equal respect and pay for the work they do, or that men shouldn't pull their weight around the house more. But start asking them about the issues that currently preoccupy feminists—abortion, for instance, or lesbian rights, or increased welfare benefits for single women, or federal day care—and many of the women they stopped would shift around uncomfortably and purse their lips. Maybe they would have strong opinions on one or all of these issues—they might be fervently pro-choice or pro-life, for example—or they might not be able to articulate why they disagree with the feminist take on these issues; or they might be embarrassed or hesitant to *say* that they disagree with that take. They may simply politely murmur something positive about all women having a "choice." But they would feel in their gut that these issues have little to do with what *they* mean by "equality" and instead veer off down a path that leads to a more radical conception of female liberation than they're comfortable with, one that doesn't have much room for men or children.

Yet if we were going to follow the logic of the women's movement to its natural end, this is the path down which we would walk—and to some degree, as the last election demonstrated, we have already begun to walk. What my generation may have discovered is that we have reached the biological limits of our freedom. Having had every legal, economic, and social impediment removed, we have run up against the impediments—if you wish to call them that—of our sex. To achieve any more, to be truly able to live the same lives as men, we'd actually have to *be* men. And this, to most women, I suspect, is not an enticing goal. Left to our own devices, we will still fall in love with men; we will continue to put our children ahead of our jobs; we will not desire, in large numbers, to become fire fighters and professional wrestlers; we will still wish to wear eye shadow and push-up bras and anything else that makes us more attractive to the opposite sex; we will, in short, continue to behave like women.

If we are going to behave otherwise—if we are going to realize the sorts of lives that feminists would have us lead, lives that are indistinguishable in every way from men's—then it's going to require a dramatic increase in the reach and ambition of the government. The feminist organizations understand this. Every one of the positions of the National Organization for Women ultimately calls upon the state to do more to enforce its view of how women should live and what they should do. If we're all going to work full-time, then we *are* going to need someone to watch our kids; twenty-four-hour, cheap, plentiful, state-run day care is the solution, as are laws that compel employers to accommodate the unpredictable emergencies of our daily lives. If divorce is easy and sex is casual, then we will need a much larger welfare program to take care of the increasing numbers of abandoned women and their children. If women do not naturally qualify for occupations like fire fighting and military combat, then we will have to lower the physical standards of these professions and impose quotas in order to recruit more women. I could go on and on. But when it comes to helping women do anything that differs from this vision—such as leaving the workforce for a spell or relying in any emotional or economic way upon men—then feminist groups are opposed. That's why, as feminist Martha Burk, president of the Center for Advancement of Public Policy, has said, feminists must be against such things as tax relief for families because that would "encourage one person to stay home and that person usually would be the woman." When asked in a radio interview what would be her way of "supporting working families through public policies," feminist economist Heidi Hartmann—president of the Institute for Women's Policy Research and winner of a MacArthur Fellowship—proposed that local public schools be turned into "eating canteens" after hours, where "[you'd] pick up your children after school, and have dinner there before you go home." State-run eating can-teens? Perhaps, too, we could use the classrooms as dormitories for work-ing families, and pretty soon the new feminist vision of a woman's life begins to look very much like the old socialist vision of everybody's life.

Many times throughout the writing of this book I've emerged from the Library of Congress on to the sunlit streets of Capitol Hill after going through some huge stack of feminist books—books that have detailed the weight of oppression women still struggle under and the utopian "gen-derless" society for which we should struggle. My head will be reeling from their litany of female misery and male discrimination: chart after chart of wage inequalities and income disparities; grim lists of nasty male traits; endless reiterations of the dogma that femininity and masculinity are social constructs that could be eliminated with enough willpower. My mouth will be dry, my head swimming, and my eyes blinking in the brightness of the daylight. As I stand outside the library getting my bear-ings, watching all the women walking swiftly by to their jobs on the Hill, or balancing sandwiches on top of their briefcases on the lawn of the Supreme Court a few doors down, or carrying on an intimate chat with their lover on a cellular phone while waiting to cross at a light, I will real-ize that nothing I have read that morning speaks to the immediacy of a woman's life. And I don't just mean my life, but any woman's life. It is like spending hours reading textbooks of Marxist theory—with its dismal vision of the oppressed working masses, its cartoonish conceptions of cap-italists in top hats and striped trousers, and its elaborate theories for world domination. Then you pass a group of construction workers with their shirts off, swapping jokes on their coffee break, and you realize that if you were to walk up to them at that moment and advance the theories you had just read, they would look at you as if you were a wandering idiot.

As I said at the beginning of this book, if we are to realize our new op-portunities, then we must recognize that the problems of women today are the problems of freedom. That's why the most embittered battles over women's issues are currently taking place among women, and not be-tween women and men. It's not only the conservative Christian women like Beverly LaHaye or Phyllis Schlafly who find themselves out of step with feminism; it is the young, professional, and educated women who find it distasteful and completely unhelpful in addressing their problems, who discover that the feminist ideas on which they were weaned do not lead them to happier lives but only to loneliness, stress, and the forfeiture of the most joyous experiences of a woman's life. These new antifeminists—or better, simply "nonfeminists"—threaten the women's movement far more than any right-wing movement, because they are the products of feminism: They have absorbed all its messages and ideas only to question and, finally, to reject them.

Feminist organizations, in reply to these women, can appeal to all sorts of very genuine grievances. But if their complaints are sometimes valid, their solutions are not. The solution, in fact, lies in the ultimate rejection of politics as a solution to one's personal problems. It lies in honestly reassessing our desires as women. It lies in truthfully acknowledging the sacrifices we have made in exchange for our current freedoms. It lies in rethinking the ways we now arrange our lives. And it lies, maybe most of all, in a readiness to reach a rapprochement with men—one based upon mutual respect for each other's differences, but also upon the mutual recognition of how much we need and desire each other.

What We Tell Our Daughters

You have won rooms of your own in the house hitherto exclusively owned by men. You are able, though not without great effort, to pay the rent. . . . But this freedom is only a beginning; the room is your own but it is still bare. It has to be furnished; it has to be decorated; it has to be shared. How are you going to furnish it, how are you going to decorate it? With whom are you going to share it and upon what terms?

VIRGINIA WOOLF, IN A 1931 SPEECH

So WHAT, in the end, do we tell our own daughters?

I brood on this question a lot, being the mother of a young girl. Many times during the course of my writing this book she has pushed open the door of my study, hung on the arm of my chair, stared into the screen of my computer, and asked, "What are you writing, Mommy?" She's still just six, and so I tell her, "Nothing you'd be interested in—not yet."

"When?"

When indeed?

Already she is thinking about what she is going to be when she grows up. On some days she tells me she wants to be a veterinarian, on others an Olympic gymnast, and still others, "a lady who makes speeches." She talks about being a mother, too, and how many children she is going to have: If she's irritated with her younger brother, she might say, "just one—a *girl*"; and if she's in a more benevolent mood, she'll announce as many as seven. I don't say much in reply except to offer her a distracted "Really?" or, "That's nice, dear." At this age she tries on identities as frequently, and as fancifully, as she does the costumes in her toy closet.

One day, though, my daughter is going to have to ask herself seriously, How am I going to do it? And, as Virginia Woolf pointedly added, *with whom . . . and upon what terms?* Not only will she want an answer, but she will want evidence that it is the right answer. What will I tell her then?

We frequently hear that there is no going back, that women have gained too much, and changed too much, to ever be satisfied again with the unworldly comforts of hearth and motherhood. But there is no going forward, either, until we establish what exactly it is we want to gain. The previous generation of women succeeded in shattering the previous assumptions about women's lives. But in the shattering, they left behind a new round of unanswered questions beginning with How? How can we be astronauts and lawyers and fighter pilots—and mothers? How can we be sexually independent—and wives? How can we demand to be treated identically to men—except for the times when we don't want to be? A beleaguered male friend of mine once joked, "It's not what the modern girl wants that matters—it's what she's going to have to settle for."

It's time to settle.

For nearly two generations women have been taught to deceive themselves about what it is they want. In the name of independence and equality, we've been told by our elders to deny our natural feelings—not to care too deeply about the men we sleep with when we're young, to suppress our longing for commitment, to delay our desire to have children, to not trust or depend upon the men to whom we finally pledge our hearts. When we do have children, we are encouraged to sacrifice them to our jobs. And if we find ourselves unhappy and dissatisfied, we've been taught to blame not the wisdom of these teachings but others—the men who have hurt us, the society that discriminates against us, the politicians who have not responded to every one of our personal needs. It is, however, the modern wisdom itself that is faulty.

At a recent party, a highly respected academic and author approached me. She knew I was writing a book about women and, having an inkling of my views, warned me not to romanticize the past too much. "I was there," she said, recalling her days in the early 1960s as a young professor struggling to earn distinction. She told me that her husband, also a professor, wrote a book at the time that won a much-coveted literary prize. She received a note of congratulations from her own college that read, "How nice [your husband] has someone as intelligent as you to talk to over breakfast." She bristled as she recalled this letter, still incensed by its patronizing tone. "That's what it was like back then," she cautioned me. We moved on to different topics, and she began telling me about her daughter, now in her thirties and also an author, who was unmarried. The woman said that she was longing for her daughter to marry and have children, although of course she respected the younger woman's choices. I began to laugh, and said, "Don't you see what you're telling me? You had to put up with a certain amount of professional disrespect and prejudice, like that letter, but you got everything else—children, a husband who is still devoted to you, and, in the end, enormous professional success, albeit success that took longer than it might have [she had spent time away from academia to raise her kids]. Today, women like me and your daughter take for granted the professional respect you craved, but we can no longer expect marriage, stability, and children when we want them. Who is the bigger loser?" And she admitted she didn't know.

Feminists like to insist that "old-fashioned values"—as garden-variety morality is now called—and the social institutions that supported them are inconsistent with modern life. Yet while it is obviously true you can't go back in time, it is not true that the teachings and principles that have guided humans since the beginning of civilization have suddenly become irrelevant. The problem we face as modern people—and particularly as modern women—is how to reconcile the old with the new. Young women today confront the daunting task of trying to plan their lives from scratch, with very little in the way of guidance about how to reconcile their modern ambitions with the old institutions of marriage and motherhood. On the one hand, they wish to be free, strong, and independent—and on the other, to find husbands who will be devoted and monogamous and will financially support them when they need it. They want to have interesting, fulfilling jobs—and yet also be involved, committed mothers. The resulting relationships are often incongruous and flimsy, like the neotraditional houses you see springing up in suburbs across America. Real estate columns explain the nostalgic return to gabled roofs, mullioned windows, and columned front porches as a desire among buyers to recapture the small, picturesque, and intimate communities that got paved over by strip malls and anonymous acres of tract housing. By bringing back some of the past's architecture, it is hoped that we can bring back some of its lost virtues as well—cozy homes teeming with family life, streets safe for children to play in, friendly neighbors who keep an eye on each other. Yet if these clusters of spanking new Colonials, Greek Revivals, and Georgians look a little incongruous in their settings—usually just a few yards away from a busy highway, with a gigantic Wal-Mart or Blockbuster looming behind them—it's because traditional structure is not so easily reconciled with modern convenience. Modern convenience, however, is something no new home buyer will do without.

The same is true in our relationships. We may pledge to love each other until death do us part—but we blanch at the first hint of sacrifice. We may believe strongly in the sanctity of marriage—but we would never impose social sanctions upon those who fail or betray their vows, or even upon couples who refuse to take those vows in the first place. As women, we may be willing to accept most of the duties of child care—but we certainly won't take sole charge of the housekeeping, and will snap at our husbands if for a moment they expect otherwise. Many of these changes in attitudes, like the advent of refrigeration and modern plumbing, seem progressive: Why should anyone stay in a marriage that is unhappy? Why should women compromise their ambitions to raise children? But, like the drywall and plywood substructures of modern houses, these attitudes have made our institutions much flimsier, and over time they endure less well.

If throughout this book I've been critical of the women's movement, it is because I see the failure of its ideals, not because I'm against, or pessimistic about, women's aspirations. I could no more oppose those than I could give up on my own daughter's education. But I do regard my daughter differently than I do my son. I know that for her to realize her dreams will take a great deal of forethought and effort, and that this effort will not be of the same kind my son will have to make. And that is not because she is less skilled or intelligent, but because her own nature will demand of her different things. Yes, I want her to be accomplished and fulfilled in her work, to be interested in the world, for her soul to be broadened by ideas, by religion, by music, and by books. But I also want her to be a wife and mother, and to experience the fulfillment and joys that come from these roles, their duties and sacrifices, their incomparable love. I want her to understand that the roles she takes on in life, in her work or family, may differ from those of men, but that they do not diminish her equality before the law or make her any less powerful in the world.

The modern feminist conception of power is actually a very narrow one. It judges women solely by their leadership in politics or the corporate world but belittles the power women have traditionally wielded in civil society: in raising the next generation; in their community, in the countless hours of unpaid work and voluntarism women devote to their neighborhoods and schools. This isn't to say that women can't be, or shouldn't strive to be, leaders. But it is to say—and this is a very old lesson—that worldly power as an end in itself does not necessarily make you happy, especially if you have sacrificed everything else in its attainment. Those women who have achieved eminence have usually had to do so at the (sometimes unwilling) sacrifice of their personal lives. It is striking how many of the great female writers did not have children; and nearly all of them, with or without children, had to sandwich their work between their domestic duties. Jane Austen wrote her novels on her lap in crowded drawing rooms, in time snatched from brooding about the price of mutton; Harriet Beecher Stowe was constantly interrupted by her children and by visits from the plumber; Sylvia Plath wrote poetry in the early hours of the morning before her children awoke, or sometimes while rocking a baby with her foot. Some female artists escaped the clutches of domesticity entirely and pursued their art by living mannish lives: George Eliot, Lillian Hellman, Mary McCarthy, Georgia O'Keeffe. But it is only women who have never had children—like Virginia Woolf and Simone de Beauvoir and so many of the feminists of our time—who could wonder why motherhood must necessarily interfere with worldly pursuits, or speculate that most women would be happier if they lived perfectly unencumbered, undistracted existences. The woman for whom work is not everything, yet who sacrifices all domestic pleasures in her pursuit of independence, may discover after a time that she has transcended not only what makes her feminine but also what makes her human.

Rather than believing in some utopian, isolated, and androgynous view of the sexes, we should take the view of Edith Wharton, who once wrote, "I have sometimes thought that a woman's nature is like a great house full of rooms." Our souls are large enough to accommodate many roles. And if we are lucky, these days most of us will live long enough to attempt everything we want. What we must now do is give serious thought as to the arrangement of these rooms. Modern feminists would ask us to put a great deal of ourselves away in the attic or basement, possibly for future use, and otherwise decorate one or two rooms (so long as it's not the kitchen!) to suit ourselves. But if our homes are going to be comfortable, expansive places, echoing with the sounds of children, with the smell of good food cooking, a warm husband in our beds, and, of course, a quiet room of our own in which to work or occasionally retreat to, then we are going to have to start planning our lives much better than we currently do.

To begin with, we are going to have to accept that simply pushing every important decision—marriage, children—to the middle of our adult lives is not only impractical but self-defeating. Right now women are leading lives that are exactly backward. We squander our youth and our sexual passion upon men who are not worth it, and only when we are older and less sexually powerful do we try and find a man who *is* worth it. We start our careers in our twenties, when we are at our most physically fertile and yet are neither old enough nor experienced enough to get anywhere professionally. Then we try to have babies when our jobs are finally starting to go somewhere but our bodies are less receptive to pregnancy. I wonder if we shouldn't consider leading our lives the other way around—modernizing, as it were, the traditional idea of getting married and having babies when our grandmothers would have, in our early twenties, and pursuing our careers later, when our children are in school.

It would, of course, be considered extremely regressive for a woman of twenty-two or twenty-three today to get married and promptly have a baby. I don't know any woman who has done it. But I wonder if it wouldn't be the most radical and even progressive act an ambitious woman could commit. Let's say she started thinking about it at the time she went to college. She could date a number of men in her late teens and early twenties, and feel less pressure to sleep with them if she knew she would soon be choosing one of them. And by taking marriage more seriously, at an earlier age, she would be less likely to waste her time, or her heart, upon men with whom she couldn't imagine spending the rest of her life. If other young women followed her example, the shrinkage in the number of sexually available young women would have its effect on men: Sexual conquests would be harder, depriving them of their current easy ability to persuade women to share their beds without sharing their lives. By marrying earlier rather than later, a woman could also have her children when she's most physically ready for them, and without too much disruption to her career, if she plans to have one.

To a modern woman, this surrender of youthful freedom might seem unimaginable. But look what she gains on the other end: By the time her second child is toddling off to nursery school, she'd still be only twenty-nine or thirty. She could have a third child if she liked; or she could enter the workforce or go to graduate school (if she hadn't already) with an easier conscience because her children would need her less than before. By the time her children were in school for a full day, she'd have just begun to hit her stride at work. She would not suddenly have to make the agonizing choice at thirty-two or thirty-three to stop everything now and drop out for a few years to have a baby—or spend six weeks with her infant and then deliver it into the hands of a nanny or day-care center. From her employer's point of view, too, the time and money invested in her training would not be spent only to see her leave at the moment she became an asset. And most of all, she would have avoided joining the hordes of thirtysomethings speaking worriedly about such things as biological clocks, career vs. motherhood, the cost of day care, infertility clinics, and the sudden shortage of available men.

Here's another unconventional idea: By marrying earlier, a woman would probably make a better marriage. There is actually little evidence to support the wisdom of our time that waiting until one is older and wiser to marry leads to happier marriages. Marriages last not just because the people within them love each other but because the time they have spent together, the events they have mutually experienced, the memories they share, and the depth of their intimacy and comfort with each other make marriage to anyone else seem impossible. If you wait to settle down until your hair is graying, when your heart is bruised, when you have seen a number of commitments you thought were true love vanish or waste away, then when you finally do marry, you may be wiser, yes, but also more broken—less willing to trust another or to make the necessary accommodations to married life. Two people who have spent their youth with each other have a better chance of growing old together; they become bound and entwined with the other like the sturdy, thick vines of wisteria, clambering up the same wall. Over time, the two souls blur together; it becomes hard to judge where she ends and he begins—a terrifying thought for a feminist, perhaps, but the essence of enduring, romantic love.

Whenever we decide to marry and have children, though, we must be willing to accept the responsibilities and sacrifices that go along with them. And this brings me to the second point in the rearrangement of our rooms. Young feminists often speak of finding a third way between feminist extremism, on the one hand, and social conservatism on the other.

Like Katie Roiphe or Naomi Wolf, they insist that women don't—or shouldn't—have to compromise their independence in marriage or when they become mothers. We should be able to keep all the perks of modern female life along with all the perks of the traditional. But this notion is not sustainable. We must understand the trade-off of every action we take. If we want to be heart surgeons or presidents, we will have to accept that we may not be the mothers we want to be, or may not be mothers at all. If we are unwilling to trust men, we might not have the marriages we want. If we refuse to give ourselves over to our families, we cannot expect much from our families in return. If we wish to live for ourselves and think only about ourselves, we will manage to retain our independence but little else.

We will also have to accept that we can't have it both ways in the larger society. If there has been one legacy of modern feminism, it has been to teach women to think of themselves as a victimized subset of humanity and not as active participants in a free and democratic society. This attitude has debased our politics, and it has poisoned the moral sensibilities of women as well. There are influential feminist writers today, like Carol Gilligan and Catharine MacKinnon, who go so far as to argue that morality and the rule of law are male constructs and are therefore unsuited to women. Women, they argue, do not accept a strict, objective understanding of right and wrong or of guilt and innocence. Women may do things that seem "wrong" from the point of view of the law, but that's only because our innately sexist society does not take into account the many good reasons a woman may be "forced" into breaking the law or why a woman, because of her different understanding of things, might not even view what she did as wrong or immoral. Actions—or at least, female actions—must be judged contextually, ideally from the point of view of the woman herself, and not by the light of abstract ethical principle. This defense has been advanced in countless criminal cases on behalf of female defendants, from those convicted of such grand crimes as murder to petty instances as shoplifting. On one memorable occasion, it prompted a former Democratic governor of Ohio, Richard F. Celeste, to pardon twenty-seven female murderers in 1990—not because these women weren't guilty, but because they claimed they'd been battered by their victims. Feminists have pleaded leniency for other women convicted of killing their lovers even in cases when there has been little evidence of abuse or when their victims were asleep at the moment they were killed. They have defended teenage mothers who drown their newborn infants or dump them in trash cans, insisting that these young women were incapable of understanding their own actions and were being held to a sentimental view of motherhood. They have excused women who have kidnapped their children to prevent their ex-husbands' access to them, acceding to the mothers' unsupported accusations that the father molested the children. Then there are women like air force pilot Kelly Flinn, who complained that she was singled out and unfairly punished for adultery even though dozens of her male colleagues had been, if less publicly, demoted or fired for the same offense (and even though the charges against her also included lying and disobeying a direct order).

The sheer familiarity of these cases, and the reflexiveness with which a female defendant will rely on such a defense for her actions, show how widely this attitude has become accepted. Its lessons are damaging—not just to public life, but to our daily lives. Women are presumed innocent, no matter what the circumstances, while men are presumed guilty. The world is unfair to women but not to men. Women should be held to lower standards of behavior and accountability, while men must be held to higher ones. In the 1997 movie *Liar, Liar*, comedian Jim Carrey, playing a lawyer, convinces his female client—a gold-digging floozy who signed a stringent prenuptial agreement—that she is entitled to half her husband's millions and custody of the children because of her status as a "victimized woman." Even though his client has had countless affairs and is to blame for the breakup of the marriage, and even though she doesn't actually *want* custody of her children but sees them only as leverage for more money, Carrey comically spins out a defense that portrays his client as a representative of all the women who have ever been persecuted by heartless, ungenerous husbands. The joke, of course, is that we are now making a joke of this defense, that we have grown cynical at the sight of otherwise strong, powerful, and fully cognizant women adopting the mantle of helpless victim to advance their interests. This cynicism is a good thing if it leads to the disappearance of these attitudes. And, frankly, they can't disappear quickly enough—not only for our daughters' sake, but for our sons' as well. It's a point as old as Socrates that human beings cannot live happily if they are unethical. The ethics that bind men must bind women, too; they are what bind us together as a just society.

Maybe what we should learn from the feminist experiment upon a generation of women is that you can't escape the consequences of your own actions. In the end, we will be judged not so much by who we are, or what we thought, as by what we did. The belief that women should bear no consequences for their decisions, that we can live independently of men and children—that we *should* live independently of them—are among the great foolish and destructive beliefs of our age, as implausible as suggesting that we should live independently of air or water. Yet in the pursuit of these beliefs, men and women alike have abandoned their responsibilities to their families and to each other. They have caused untold pain and unhappiness to their children as well as to themselves. But men and women should not be locked in competition: One sex cannot triumph over the other without hurting itself. Men and women are as inextricably linked and necessary to one another as the food we eat and the children we bear to replace the dead.

I hope for so many things for my daughter, but I hope above all that she understands this: that her fulfillment in life will come from knowing that she did not only what was right for herself but what was right for the people she loved, which in turn will be right for society as a whole. In understanding this, she will achieve more than merely a room of her own. She will be able, in the freest and best of eras in all of history, to have as many rooms as she likes, so many that she may have rooms that she won't even know what to do with yet.

This might seem like very ancient advice. That's what makes it all the more revolutionary today. Sometimes the job of a mother is simply to repeat the old truths again and again and again, and pray that they stick.

Index

About the Author

Danielle Crittenden is the founding editor of *The Women's Quarterly* magazine, published by the Independent Women's Forum in Washington, D.C. She has written for *The Wall Street Journal, The New York Times, The Washington Post,* the *Weekly Standard,* and the *Ladies' Home Journal,* among other publications. She is also a frequent commentator on women's issues for national television and radio. Crittenden was born in Toronto, Canada, in 1963. She lives in Washington, D.C., with her husband and two children.